JEREMIAH

Priest and Prophet

JEREMIAH

Priest and Prophet

By

F. B. Meyer, B.A.

CHRISTIAN • LITERATURE • CRUSADE
Fort Washington, Pennsylvania 19034

CHRISTIAN LITERATURE CRUSADE

U.S.A.
P.O. Box 1449, Fort Washington, PA 19034

BRITAIN
51 The Dean, Alresford, Hants SO24 9BJ

AUSTRALIA
P.O. Box 91, Pennant Hills N.S.W. 2120

NEW ZEALAND
126 Broadway, Palmerston North

First American edition 1980

This revised edition 1993

Cover picture: SuperStock

ISBN   0-87508-355-2

PRINTED IN THE UNITED STATES OF AMERICA

CONTENTS

Most of the Scripture quotes herein are taken either from the King James or the 1881 Revised Version. However, the author sometimes uses his own paraphrases.

PREFACE TO THE ORIGINAL EDITION

JEREMIAH has always a fascination to Christian hearts because of the close similarity that exists between his life and that of Jesus Christ. Each of them was "a man of sorrows, and acquainted with grief"; each came to his own, and his own received him not; each passed through hours of rejection, desolation, and forsakeness. And in Jeremiah we may see beaten out into detail, experiences which, in our Lord, are but lightly touched on by the evangelists.

It is by no means an easy task to discern the true order of Jeremiah's prophecies. The clue to their present arrangement seems lost. Probably the chapters are grouped more according to subject than to chronology, those touching on the same topic being grouped together. In this book I have endeavored, as far as possible, to follow the chronological sequence.

If I had been writing a history of the last days of the monarchy of Judah, these pages would have been much extended; but I have refrained from this, wishing only to tell so much of the general story as was needful to elucidate the part Jeremiah was called to play.

It will more than serve my purpose if I shall be able to make the personality of this great man more familiar to the general Christian public. For some reason there is a great amount of ignorance of the life and times of Jeremiah which contrasts remarkably with the veneration with which the Jews have always regarded him. But amid the names that shine as stars in the hemisphere of

Old Testament Scripture there is not one more brilliant than his.

There is a special message in the ministry of Jeremiah for those who are compelled to stand alone, who fall into the ground to die, who fill up what is behind of the sufferings of Christ, and through death arise to bear fruit in the great world of men, which they passionately love.

F.B. MEYER

1

"THE WORD OF THE LORD CAME UNTO ME"

(JEREMIAH 1:4, 12, 13)

> We know things that we cannot say;
> We soar where we could never map our flight;
> We see flashes and colorings too quick and bright
> For any hand to paint. We hear
> Strange far-off mental music, all too sweet,
> Too great for any earthly instrument;
> Gone, if we strive to bring it near.
>
> F. R. Havergal

IF the days of David and Solomon may be compared to spring and summer in the history of the Kingdom of Israel, it was late autumn when our story opens. The influence of the spiritual revival under Hezekiah and Isaiah, which had for a brief interval arrested the process of decline, had spent itself; and not even the reforms of the good king Josiah, which affected rather the surface than the heart of the people, would avail to avert inevitable judgment.

The northern tribes were captive on the plains of Mesopotamia, whence, in the dawn of history, their race had sprung. And Judah, unwarned by the fate of her sister Israel, was rapidly pursuing the same path, to be presently involved in a similar catastrophe. King and court, princes and people, prophets and priests, were infected with the abominable vices for which the Canaanites had been expelled from the Promised Land centuries before.

Every high hill had its thick grove of green trees, within whose shadow the idolatrous rites and abominable license of nature worship were freely practiced. The face of the country was thickly covered with temples erected for the worship of Baal and Astarte, and all the host of heaven, and with lewd idols. In the cities, the black-robed *chemarim*, the priests of these unhallowed practices, flitted to and fro in strange contrast to the white-stoled priests of Jehovah. The people were taught to consider vice as part of their religion, and to frequent houses dedicated to impurity. All kinds of evil thrived unchecked. The poor were plundered, the innocent falsely accused; wicked men lay in wait to catch men; theft and murder, adultery and idolatry, like spores of corruption, filled the fetid air and flourished on the tainted soil (2:20, 27, 34; 5:7-8, 26; 9:2).

But it was in Jerusalem that these evils came to a head. In the streets of the holy city, the children were taught to gather wood while the fathers kindled the fire and the women kneaded dough to make cakes for Astarte, "the queen of heaven," and to pour out drink offerings unto other gods. The Temple, with so many sacred associations, was the headquarters of Baal worship; its courts were desecrated by monstrous images and symbols, and its precincts were the abode of infamous men and women. It seemed as though the king of Sodom had dispossessed Melchizedek in his ancient home. Below the Temple battlements, deep down in the valley of Hinnom, scenes were constantly witnessed that recalled the darkest cruelties of heathendom. There was the high place of Tophet, which derived its name from the clamor of the drums that drowned the cries of the babes flung into the fires. It was an awful combination. "The Temple of the Lord, the Temple of the Lord!" was the cry of the heartless formalist; while below the sacred shrine such scenes of devilry were rife. Ah me! Would that it had been the last time in the world's history when the profession of true religion had been accompanied by the license of vice and the service of the devil!

In such a Sodom, God's voice must be heard. The Judge of all the earth must warn the ungodly of a certain retribution—only to be averted by swift repentance. The Good Shepherd must seek his wayward sheep. Better believe that there is no God than think that he could be speechless in the presence of sins that frustrated his election and long education of Israel, and threatened to terminate its very existence as a people.

Yet if God speak, it must be through the yielded lips of man. For if his voice struck the ear of sinful man directly, it would either paralyze him with dread or seem indistinct, like the mutterings of thunder. Therefore in every age the Divine Spirit has gone through the world, seeking for the prepared lip of elect souls through which to utter himself. He seeks such today. Men are still the vehicles of his communications to men. To us, as to Ezekiel, the Divine Spirit says, "Son of man, thou shalt hear the word at my mouth, and give them warning from me."

In the call of Jeremiah we may discover the sort of man whom God chooses as the medium for his speech. And our discovery will greatly startle us. We shall find the heavenly treasure in a simple earthen vessel. Not in the metropolis, but in the poor village of Anathoth, three miles to the north; not in an elder, but in a youth; not among the high and noble, but in the family of an undistinguished priest; not in a man mighty as Elijah, eloquent as Isaiah, or seraphic as Ezekiel; but in one who was timid and shrinking, conscious of his helplessness, yearning for a sympathy and love he was never to know—such was the chosen organ through which the word of the Lord came to that corrupt and degenerate age.

It is not to be expected that a superficial gaze will discern the special qualifications that attracted the divine choice to Jeremiah. But that is no wonder. The instruments of the divine purpose in all ages had not been such as man would have selected. God has always chosen "the foolish things of the world, that he might put to shame them that are wise; and the weak things of the world, that he might put to shame the things that are strong; and the base things of the world, and the things that are despised, yea, and the things that are not, that he might bring to nought the things that are; that no flesh should glory before God." Your family may be poor in Manasseh, and yourself the least in your father's house—nothing more than a cake of barley bread: yet if God lay hold of you, he will work a wonderful deliverance.

But there were several reasons why Jeremiah might have been passed over.

He was young. How young we do not know; but young enough for him to start back at the divine proposal with the cry, "Ah, Lord God! Behold, I cannot speak; for I am a child." Without doubt, as a boy he had enjoyed peculiar advantages. He came of a priestly family; his father, Hilkiah, may have been the high priest who, in the discharge of his sacred office in the Temple, discovered the manuscript roll which proved to be a copy of the Book of the Law, and led to the reformation under Josiah. His uncle, Shallum, was the husband of Huldah the prophetess, in whom the fire of the old Hebrew faith was burning brightly even in those days of almost universal degeneracy. Shaphan, Baruch, and Hanameel were probably the companions of his youth, and afterwards formed a little band, who nourished the noblest traditions of the national life. Still, Jeremiah was but as a child.

God has often selected the young for posts of eminent service: Samuel and Timothy; Joseph and David; Daniel and John the Baptist; Calvin, who wrote his *Institutes* before he was twenty-four; and Wesley, who was only twenty-five when he inaugurated the great system of Methodism. In every age of the Church young eyes have eagerly scanned this paragraph—and have dared to cherish the hope that since youth did not disqualify Jeremiah, so it would not render them unfit for the special service of God. The only thing to be sure of is that God has really called you; and this can only be ascertained after very careful consideration. There is first the consciousness of a strong inward impulse, which is most present in the holiest hours but which is never far away, and often surges up pure and strong in the soul. There is next a certain concurrence of providence by which other doors seem closed and that opened which conducts to the desired goal. Besides these, there is a natural adaptation, a consensus of opinion among friends and advisers, and the constant voice of the Spirit through the Word.

He was naturally timid and sensitive. By nature he seemed cast in too delicate a mold to be able to combat the dangers and difficulties of his time. He reminds us of a denizen of the sea, accustomed to live within its shell, but suddenly deprived of its strong encasement and thrown without covering on the sharp edges of the rocks. The bitter complaint of his later life was that his mother had brought him into a world of strife and contention. And it was in allusion to the natural shrinking of his disposition that Jehovah promised to make him a "defensed city, an iron pillar, and a brazen wall against the whole land."

Many are molded upon this type. They have the sensitiveness of a girl, and the nervous organism of a gazelle. They love the shallows, with their carpet of silver sand, rather than the strong billows that test a man's endurance. For them, it is enough to run with footmen; they have no desire to contend with horses. They love the land of peace in which they are secure, and have no heart for the swelling of Jordan. Yet such, like Jeremiah, may play a heroic part on the world's stage, if only they will let God lay down the iron of his might along the lines of their natural weakness. His strength is only made perfect in weakness. It is to those who have no might that he increaseth strength. Happy is the soul that can look up from its utter helplessness and say with Jeremiah, "O Lord, my strength in the day of affliction"; or with Micah, in yet earlier times, "Truly I am full of power, by the Spirit of the Lord, and of judgment, and of might, to declare unto Jacob his transgression, and to Israel his sin."

He particularly shrank from the burden he was summoned to bear. His chosen theme would have been God's mercy—the boundlessness of his compassion, the tenderness of his pity. In the earlier chapters, when pleading with the people to return to God, there is a tenderness in his voice and pathos in his speech, which proves how thoroughly his heart was in this part of his work. Some of his choicest allusions to natural scenes are intended to set forth the love of God to backsliding and penitent souls. God's mercy is like "a fountain of living waters," as contrasted to the brackish contents of the rock-hewn cisterns; or like the ocean waves lapping on the bank of soft sand they may not pass; or like a husband's great love, which cannot forget the day of espousals amid the unfaithfulness which has ruined the peace of his home.

But to be charged with a message of judgment; to announce the woeful day; to oppose every suggestion of heroic resistance; to charge home on the prophetic and the priestly orders (to each of which he belonged, and the anger of each of which he incurred) the crimes by which they were disgraced—this was the commission that was furthest from his choice. "As for me," he cried, "I have not hastened from being a shepherd after thee; neither have I desired the woeful day; thou knowest" (17:16, R.V.).

He was conscious of his deficiency in speech. Like Moses, he could say, "O Lord, I am not eloquent, neither heretofore nor since thou has spoken unto thy servant: but I am slow of speech, and of a slow tongue." Like Isaiah, he might cry, "Woe is me! For I am undone:

because I am a man of unclean lips, and I dwell in the midst of a people of unclean lips: for mine eyes have seen the King, the Lord of Hosts." Like the Apostle Paul, he would affirm, "My speech and my preaching were not in persuasive words of wisdom." "Then said I, Ah, Lord God! Behold, I cannot speak; for I am a child."

The best speakers for God are frequently they who are least gifted with human eloquence; for if that be richly present—the mighty power of moving men—there is an imminent peril of relying on it, and attributing the results to its magnetic spell. God cannot give his glory to another. He may not share his praise with man. He dare not expose his servants to the temptation of sacrificing to their own net or trusting their own ability. Of God, and through God, and to God, must be all things, that the glory may be his forever.

Do not then despair because of these apparent dis-qualifications. None of them will shut out from you the accents of the voice of God. Notwithstanding all, the word of the Lord shall come to you; not for your sake alone, but for those to whom you shall be sent. The one thing that God demands of you is absolute consecration to his purpose, and willingness to go on any errand on which he may send you. If these are yours, all else will be given you. He will hush your alarm—"Be not afraid!" He will assure you of his presence—"I am with thee, to deliver thee." He will equip you—"Then the Lord put forth his hand, and touched my mouth; and the Lord said unto me, Behold, I have put my words in thy mouth." How the word of the Lord came to Jeremiah we cannot tell; whether audibly as to Samuel, or in the deep chambers of his soul. But when it came, he knew it. And we shall know it. Oh for the circumcised ear, and the loyal, obedient heart!

2

"I FORMED THEE"

(JEREMIAH 1:5)

I was not born
Informed and fearless from the first, but shrank
From aught which marked me out apart from men:
I would have lived their life, and died their death,
Lost in their ranks, eluding destiny.
                                                    Browning

GOD has a plan for each of his children. From the foot of the cross, where we are cradled in our second birth, to the brink of the river, where we lay down our armor, there is a path which he has prepared for us to walk in. Its roughness and steeps, its velvet grass and quiet glades, its climb up the mountainside and descent into the valley of dark shadow—have all been planned and laid out by his matchless wisdom, his unerring love. The path has been prepared; it is for us to walk in it.

On the other hand, God prepares *us* for the path he has chosen. We are his workmanship, created unto the good works which he has before prepared. There is no emergency in the path for which there has not been provision made in our nature; and there is no faculty stored in our nature which, sooner or later, shall not have its proper exercise and use. From the earliest inception of being, God had a plan for Jeremiah's career, for which he prepared him. Before the dawn of consciousness, in the very origin of his nature, the hands of the great Master Workman reached down out of heaven to shape the plastic clay for the high purpose which he had in view. Note the conjunction of those two expressions: I *appointed and sanctified* thee a prophet to the nations; and again, I *formed* thee. God always forms those whom he has appointed and sanctified for any great work.

Ask what your work in the world is. That for which you were born, to which you were appointed, on account of which you were conceived in the creative thought of God. That there is a divine purpose in your being is indubitable. Seek that you may be permitted to realize it. And never doubt that you have been endowed with all the special aptitudes which that purpose may demand. God has formed you for it, storing your mind with all that he knew to be requisite for your lifework. It is your part to elaborate and improve to the utmost the two talents which you have. Do not envy another his five. Those three additional ones were not needed for the special purpose that you were designed to fulfill. And it is enough to answer the divine intention in your creation, redemption, or call to service, whatever it may have been. Do not be jealous or covetous; it is enough for you to be what God made you to be, and to be always at your best.

1. THE DIVINE PURPOSE. *I knew thee . . . I sanctified thee . . . I have appointed thee a prophet.* In that degenerate age the great Lover of souls needed a spokesman; and the divine decree determined the conditions of Jeremiah's birth, and character, and life. How this could be consistent with the exercise of personal volition and choice on the part of the youthful prophet, we cannot say. We can only see the two piers of the mighty arch, but not the arch itself, since the mists of time veil it, and we are dim of sight. Some try to explain it by introducing the thought of foreknowledge; they quote the words, "Whom God did

foreknow he also did predestinate." But, after all, this only carries the difficulty one step further back into mystery.

It is wise to ascertain, if possible, while life is yet young, the direction of the divine purpose. There are four considerations that will help us. First, the indication of our natural aptitudes; for these, when touched by the Divine Spirit, become talents or gifts. Secondly, the inward impulse or energy of the Divine Spirit, working in us both to will and to do his good pleasure. Thirdly, the teaching of the Word of God. Fourthly, the evidence of the circumstances and demands of life. When these concur, and focus in one point, there need be no doubt as to the divine purpose and plan. It was thus that God disclosed to Samuel, and Jeremiah, and Saul of Tarsus, the future for which they were destined. And it is extremely delightful when, from the first bud of youth to the flower and fruit of maturity, the heavenly vision has molded the entire tenor and development of the life.

But in cases where the divine purpose is not so clearly disclosed, in which life is necessarily lived piece-meal, and the bits of marble for the tesselated floor are heaped together with no apparent plan, we must dare to believe that God has an intention for each of us; and that if we are true to our noblest ideals, we shall certainly work out the divine pattern and be permitted some day to see it in its unveiled symmetry and beauty. Perhaps the noblest aim for any of us is to realize that word which, according to the margin of the Revised Version, was addressed by God to Jeremiah, "On whatsoever errand I shall send thee, thou shalt go; and whatsoever I shall command thee, thou shalt speak" (1:7).

To run errands for God! To be like the angels that excel in strength, and do his commandment, hearkening to the voice of his word! To resemble the boy messengers in some of our large cities, that wait in readiness to discharge any commission that may be entrusted to them! To know that your message is as certainly given you as the letter which is placed under the wing of the carrier pigeon! To go on occupying the position in which we have been placed by the providence of God, and to hold it for God until he bids us do something else! Such are golden secrets of blessedness and usefulness.

2. FORMATIVE INFLUENCES. It is very interesting to study the formative influences that were brought to bear on the character of Jeremiah. There were the character and disposition of his mother, and the priestly office of his father. There was the picturesque beauty of his birthplace, the village of Anathoth, on the main road three miles north of Jerusalem, encircled by the famous hills of Benjamin, and looking down the ravine on the blue waters of the Dead Sea gleaming at the foot of the purple hills of Moab. There was the near proximity of the holy city, rendering it possible for the boy to be present at all the holy festivals, and to receive such instruction as the best seminaries could provide. There was the companionship and association of godly families, like those of Shaphan and Maaseiah, who themselves had passed away but whose children preserved the religion of their forefathers and treasured as sacred relics the literature, psalms, and history of purer and better days. His uncle, Shallum, was the husband of the illustrious and devoted prophetess, Huldah; and their son Hanameel shared with Baruch, the grandson of Maaseiah, the close friendship of the prophet—probably from the days that they were boys together. There were also the prophets Nahum and Zephaniah, who were burning as bright constellations in that dark sky, to be soon joined by himself.

His mind was evidently very sensitive to all the influences of his early life. His speech is saturated with references to natural emblems and national customs, to the life of men and the older literature of the Bible. Take, for instance, his earliest sermon in which he refers to the story of the Exodus and the pleadings of

Deuteronomy; to the roar of the young lion and the habits of the wild ass; to the young camel traversing her ways and the Arabian of the wilderness; to the murmur of the brook and the hewing of the cistern. His quick and sensitive soul eagerly incorporate the influences of the varied life around him and reproduce them. Many fabrics weave into the texture of his mind. Many flowers mingle their perfume in the enclosure of his heart. Many chords make up the music of his speech.

It is thus that God is ever at work, forming and molding us. Whenever you are called to pass through an experience which is unusually trying and difficult, comfort yourself by the thought that you are being fitted for some high purpose that has not yet been made known, but which will lay its demand on that very experience which has been permitted for that end. And, as you look back on your life, you will see how all has been ordered to fit you to fulfill a ministry to others that would have been less worthily fulfilled had you been excused from the tears, the hardships, the privations of a single day. The plan of God threads the maze of life. The purpose of God gives meaning to many of its strange experiences. Be brave, strong and trustful! If God serves himself through you, he will recompense you. He is not unfaithful to forget.

There is a striking illustration of this in one of the closing scenes of Joseph's life. Speaking to his brethren of the pit, and the afflictions to which it led, he said, "Ye meant it for evil; but God meant it for good" (Gen. 50:20). Standing on the eminence of the years, he was able to read God's meaning in that dark and mysterious providence. And if he had been asked to state his view of the divine reason in the trials and hardships of those early days, fast fading behind the mist of years, he would probably have answered, "God was forming me for my future; preparing me for what he had prepared for me; disciplining and equipping me for the position that awaited me; and there is no single incident in all those weary years through which I passed that I could have dispensed with except at a serious disadvantage to my present standing."

3. THERE WAS ALSO A SPECIAL PREPARATION AND ASSURANCE FOR HIS LIFEWORK. "The Lord put forth his hand, and touched my mouth. And the Lord said unto me, Behold, I have put my words in thy mouth" (1:9). In a similar manner had the seraph touched the lips of Isaiah years before. And we are reminded that the Lord Jesus promised that the Spirit of the Father would put appropriate words into the lips of his disciples when summoned before the tribunals of their foes. Words are the special gift of God. They were the endowment of the Church at Pentecost. And speaking as the Spirit gives utterance always evidences a Spirit-filled man.

God never asks us to go on his errands (1:7) without telling us what to say. If we are living in fellowship with him, he will impress his messages on our minds and enrich our lives with the appropriate utterances by which those messages shall be conveyed to our fellows. Do any read these words who, like Moses, lack this royal endowment—their words fall pointless and dead? Let them offer their lips to speak, not with the wisdom of human words nor with the grace of human eloquence but with the power and demonstration of the Holy Ghost—their appeal will not be denied. If only God's glory be our object, God's hand will be put forth to touch our mouth and he will leave his words there.

Two other assurances were also given. First, "Thou shalt go to whomsoever I shall send thee." This gave a definiteness and directness to the prophet's speech. Secondly, "Be not afraid because of them; for I am with thee to deliver thee, saith the Lord" (1:8, R.V.). An assurance which was remarkably fulfilled, as we shall see, in the unfolding of this narrative.

These are marvelous words, spoken to us all as God sends us on a mission, or errand, into the world. It may be of greater or less consequence—to rule an empire or nurse a single babe, to be an apostle or to care for a few sheep in the wilderness. But we are no less sent than Jesus was from the bosom of the Father—sent to learn, sent to suffer, sent to achieve. Sent on an errand as Joseph was from the patriarchal tent.

And, just as long as we are on the prepared path, performing the appointed mission, God is with us. We may defy death. We bear a charmed life. We are more than conquerors. The music of his voice sounds in our heart though defaming and terror are on every side (20:10). Men may fight against us, but they cannot prevail; for the Lord of Hosts is with us, the God of Jacob is our refuge (1:19).

4. LASTLY, GOD VOUCHSAFED A TWOFOLD VISION TO HIS CHILD (vs. 11–16). On the one hand, the swift-blossoming almond tree assured him that God would watch over him and see to the swift performance of his predictions; on the other, the seething cauldron, turned towards the north, indicated the breaking out of evil. So the pendulum of life swings to and fro; now to light and then to dark. But happy is the man whose heart is fixed, trusting in the Lord. He is hidden in the secret of God's pavilion from the strife of tongues; and abides in the secret place of the tabernacles of the Most High. Men may fight against him but they shall not prevail; he is encircled in the environing care of Jehovah; he is as safe as the Israelites when the cloud lay between them and Pharaoh. As God spoke to Jeremiah, so he addresses us: "They shall fight against thee, but they shall not prevail against thee; for I am with thee, saith the Lord, to deliver thee" (1:19). "We are immortal until our work is done."

There was a period in Jeremiah's life when he seems to have swerved from the pathway of complete obedience (15:19) and to have gone back from following the God-given plan. Surrounded by contention and strife; cursed as though he were a usurer; reproached and threatened with death—he lost heart and fainted in the precipitous path. Immediately he had good reason to fear that the divine protection had been withdrawn. We are only safe when we are on God's plan. But as Jeremiah returned again to his allegiance, God's precious promises were renewed and again sounded in his ears: "I will make thee unto this people a fenced brazen wall; and they shall fight against thee, but they shall not prevail against thee; for I am with thee to save thee and to deliver thee, saith the Lord. And I will deliver thee out of the hand of the wicked, and I will redeem thee out of the hand of the terrible" (vs. 20–21).

It may be that you have stepped back before some fearful storm of opposition, as a fireman before the belching flames. Thus Cranmer signed his recantation. Yet return again to your post; renew your protest; take forth the precious from the vile. The old blessing will flood your soul; God will bring you again that you may stand before him, and you shall be as his mouth. Thus it was with Peter on the day of Pentecost.

3

CISTERN MAKING

(JEREMIAH 2:13)

Attempt, how vain—
With things of earthly sort, with aught but God
With aught but moral excellence, truth and love—
To satisfy and fill the immortal soul!
To satisfy the ocean with a drop;
To marry immortality to death;
And with unsubstantial slave of time
To fill the embrace of all eternity.

Pollok's *Course of Time*

THERE was probably little interval between Jeremiah's call and his entrance upon his sacred work. Once the Spirit of God has established a code of communications between himself and the soul whom he has selected to be his mouthpiece, he is likely to avail himself of it constantly. The difficulty is to lay down the wire through the ocean depths; but when it is there, the messages flash to and fro repeatedly. So we are told that to this young, ardent soul "the word of the Lord came" (2:1). Coming, it thrilled him.

He dwelt but lightly on the ominous mention of the inevitable conflict which the divine voice prognosticated. He did not stay to gauge the full pressure of opposition indicated in the celestial storm-signal. He had been told that kings and princes, priests and people, would fight against him; but in the first blush of his young faith he thought more of the presence of Jehovah, who had promised to make him "a defensed city, an iron pillar and brazen walls against the whole land." How tenderly God veils our future and leads us forward step by step! But there is a difference between the elastic hopefulness of youth and the experience of manhood. The earlier chapters of Jeremiah differ from his Lamentations as does the first green of spring from the sere foliage of autumn.

As we study the words and deeds of this most human of prophets, let us pass through his plaintive cries and tears and prayers to that Divine Man, whose gentle spirit was so closely anticipated and reflected in that of his servant. In every age God is at work through his servants, striving against sin in every form, and seeking to set up his reign of righteousness, peace, and joy. In Jeremiah's words we have his vehement beseechings and remonstrances; in Jeremiah's prayers we have echoes of the unutterable intercessions of the Holy Spirit; in Jeremiah's conflicts we have the divine antagonism against flesh and blood, and the rulers of the darkness of this world; in Jeremiah's laments we have the divine grief over human willfulness. This priest and prophet of the Jerusalem of David and Solomon had a remarkable course to pursue in presenting, in the obscure mirror of his life, the cross and sorrow of the true Priest and Prophet of the restored Jerusalem.

1. THE PROPHET'S TWOFOLD BURDEN. When Jeremiah began his ministry, going from Anathoth to Jerusalem for that purpose (2:2), Josiah, though only twenty-one years of age, had been thirteen years on the throne. He was commencing those measures of reform which availed to postpone, though not avert, the doom of city and nation. His measures were as drastic as those of Cromwell and his soldiers in their determined effort to

remove every vestige of popery from churches and public buildings. "They brake down the altars of the Baalim in his presence; and the sun-images, that were on high above them, he hewed down; and the Asherim, and the graven images, and the molten images, he brake in pieces, and made dust of them, and strewed it upon the graves of them that had sacrificed unto them. And he burnt the bones of the priests upon their altars, and purged Judah and Jerusalem" (2 Chron. 34:4–5, R.V.).

There must have been a great cawing among the rooks when the trees in which they had so long nested were felled. For seventy years the grossest forms of idolatry had held almost undisputed sway. The impious orgies and degrading rites, which licensed vice as a part of religion, were in harmony with the depraved tastes of the people. What, therefore, ecclesiastics and their flocks felt towards Henry VIII when he demolished the monasteries, and to the Protector when his officers pursued their work of devastation, must have found ready place in those early years of Josiah's reign.

The result was—first, that the work of reform was largely superficial; it did not strike beneath the surface, nor change the trend of national choice. And secondly, this policy compacted together a strong political party determined to promote a closer alliance with Egypt which, under Psammetichus, had just asserted her independence against the king of Assyria. In these two directions the young prophet was called to make his influence felt.

First, he protested against the prevalent sin around him. The one thought of the people was to preserve the outward acknowledgment of Jehovah by the maintenance of the Temple services and rites. If these were rigorously observed, they considered that there was no sufficient cause for charging them with the sin of apostasy. They insisted that they were not polluted (2:23); and reiterated with wearisome monotony, "The Temple of the Lord, the Temple of the Lord, the Temple of the Lord, are these" (7:4).

It was Jeremiah's mission to show that mere outward observance was worse than useless, compatible with a real forsaking of God. Like the flush of hectic fever, it only concealed the corruption eating its way into the heart. Like the flowers on the edge of the precipice, it hid the fatal brink. Nominal profession is compatible with utter atheism; and with the worst form of atheism, because the heart parries every attack with the foil of apparent and avowed belief.

This will account for the plain denunciations of sin that came burning hot from the lips of the young prophet. He includes the priests and expounders of the law, pastors and prophets, in his scathing words (2:8). The valley of Hinnom, with its obscene and cruel rites, is quoted in evidence against them (v. 23). The blood of children flung into the fires is detected on their robes (v. 34); the trees of the groves whisper what they have witnessed beneath their shadow; and the jagged rocks tell stories they dare not conceal (20; 3:6). Every metaphor is adopted that human art can suggest to bring home to the people their infidelity to their great Lover and Redeemer, God (3:20).

He also protested against the proposal to form an Egyptian alliance. The little land of Canaan lay between the vast rival empires founded on the Nile and the Euphrates, much as Switzerland between France and Austria. Therefore, it was constantly exposed to the transit of immense armies, like locusts destroying everything, or to the hostile incursions of one or other of its belligerent neighbors. It had always been the policy of a considerable party at the court of Jerusalem to cultivate alliance with Egypt or Assyria. In Hezekiah's and Manasseh's time the tendency had been towards Assyria; now it was towards Egypt which had, in a remarkable way, thrown off the yoke which the great king Esarhaddon in three terrible campaigns had sought to rivet on its neck. The prophet strenuously opposed these overtures. Why should his people bind themselves to the fortunes of

any heathen nation whatsoever? Was not
King? Would not he succor them in times of
calamity? Surely their true policy was to stand alone,
untrammeled by foreign alliances, resting only on the
mighty power of Jehovah, serving his purposes, true to
his law, devoted to his will. "What hast thou to do in the
way of Egypt, to drink the waters of Sihor [*i.e.*, the Black
Nile]; or what hast thou to do in the way of Assyria, to
drink the waters of the river?" (2:18, 36–37).

This, then, was Jeremiah's mission—to stand almost
alone; to protest against the sins of the people which
were covered by their boasted reverence to Jehovah,
whom they worshiped as the tutelary deity of their land
alongside many false gods—and to oppose the policy of
the court, which sought to cultivate friendly relations
with the one power that seemed able to render aid to his
fatherland in the awful struggle with the northern kingdom which he saw to be imminent (1:15). And this
ministry was exercised in the teeth of the most virulent
opposition. Here was a priest denouncing the practices
of priests, a prophet the lies of prophets. It was no light
thing to expose the falsehoods alike of priest and
prophet, and accuse them of healing the hurt of the
daughter of his people slightly, saying, "Peace, peace,"
when there was no peace. Small wonder, therefore, that
the most powerful parties in the state conspired against
him, as in later days when Pilate and Herod would join
hands against Christ.

2. THE IMAGERY HE EMPLOYED. It is a scene among the
mountains. In that green glade a fountain rises icy cold
from the depths and pours its silver stream downward
through the valley. You can hear the music of its ripple
and trace its course by the vegetation that follows it. It
is always flowing in abundance for young and old, for
the villagers in the hamlets and, when it has grown
fuller and broader, for the inhabitants of large towns
along its course. But its banks are unvisited; neither

cup nor bucket descends into its crystal depths. For all practical purposes it might as well cease to flow.

Far away from that verdant valley you hear the clink of the chisel, and presently discover people of every age and rank engaged in making cisterns to supply their homes. The bead-drops stand thick upon their brow, as from early dawn to far on into the night they pursue their arduous toil, wrestling with the stubborn granite. They will not avail themselves of the materials of former times, nor utilize the half-hewn cisterns deserted by their ancestors. Each man has his own scheme, his own design. He toils at it when spring casts her green mantle over the pasture lands that come to the edge of the quarry, and when the summer heat makes the quarry like a kiln. While people elsewhere are gathering in ripe grapes or golden corn, he remains constant to his toil, and he is there amid the biting cold of winter. After years of work he may achieve his purpose, and complete the cistern on which he has spent his years. He calls on his neighbors to view his accomplished purpose and waits expectant of the shower. Presently it descends, and he is filled with pride and pleasure to think of the store of water which he has been able to secure. But lo! it does not stay! As soon as it enters, it passes out. There is a fatal crack or flaw; perhaps the stone is too porous. He finds, what every one of his neighbors has found, or will find—that even with the utmost care the cisterns wrought in the quarry can hold no water.

What an infinite mistake to miss the fountain freely flowing to quench the thirst, and hew out the broken cistern in which is disappointment and despair! Yet this, said the prophet, was the precise position of Israel. They had done as no other nation, though searches were made from the far west of Chittim to the far east of Kedar. The heathen at least were constant to their gods. False religions were indigenous to the lands where they had originated—the same idols worshiped, the same rites performed, the same temples filled with succeeding generations. But the people of Jehovah had forsaken him, as a maid might lay aside her ornaments or a bride her attire; and in resorting to false religions and heathen alliances, they were hewing out for themselves broken cisterns which would fail them in their hour of need.

Very pathetically the prophet reminds them of the past. The kindness of their youth, the love of their espousals, their holiness to the Lord, and the song with which they celebrated their deliverance on the shores of the Red Sea, all suggest a sad contrast to the evils that curse the land. Through him the voice of God is heard inquiring the reason of this lamentable apostasy. The chapter is full of questions, as though God would elicit the charge upon which they had deserted him. "What unrighteousness have your fathers found in me, that they are gone far from me, and have walked after vanity and are become vain? Have I been a wilderness unto Israel? Or a land of thick darkness? Wherefore say my people, We are broken loose, we will come no more unto thee?"

There is nothing sadder than the ebb of love, when we are compelled to sit on the beach and watch the slowly receding waters as they drop down from the high water mark which they had reached with the dancing wavelets. This takes the light from the eye and the spring from the foot. Life can never again be quite as it was. The tide may come up again, but it will never efface the recollection of the ebb and the fear of its return. This in human experience is something like the pain felt by the Eternal as he saw Israel, for whom he had done so much, turn from him to strangers. Bitter, indeed, to hear them say to a stock, "Thou art my father"; and to a stone, "Thou hast brought me forth." Their apostasy was to God as a wife leaving the husband who dotes upon her to become another man's wife (3:1).

3. ITS APPLICATION TO OURSELVES. Many cistern-makers may read these words—each with soul-thirst craving

satisfaction, each within easy reach of God, whose nature is as rock-water for those that are athirst. But all attempting the impossible task of satisfying the thirst for the Infinite and Divine with men and things.

There is the cistern of *pleasure*, embroidered with fruits and flowers, and bacchanalian figures, wrought at the cost of health and rest; the cistern of *wealth*, gilded and inlaid with pearls, like the mangers of the stud of Eastern kings; the cistern of *fame*, hewn by the youth who tore himself from the welcome of home and the embrace of human love, to climb, with his banner of strange device, the unfrequented solitudes of the mountain summit, far above all rivalry, and even companionship; the cistern of *human love* which, however beautiful as a revelation of the divine love, can never satisfy the soul that rests in it alone. All of these, made at infinite cost of time and pains, deceive and disappoint. In the expressive words of Jeremiah, they are "broken cisterns that can hold no water." And in the time of trouble they will not be able to save those that have constructed and trusted them.

At your feet, O weary cistern-hewer, the fountain of God's love is flowing through the channel of the Divine Man! Stoop to drink it. We must descend to the level of the stream if its waters are to flow over our parched lips to slake our thirst. You have already dropped your tools and are weary of your toil. Listen to the music that fills the air and floats around, like the chime of angel voices: "Come back to God. Do the first works. Forsake the alliances and idolatries which have alienated you from your best Friend. Open your heart, that he may create in you the fountain of living water, leaping up to eternal life. . . . The Spirit and the bride say, Come! And he that heareth, let him say, Come! And he that is athirst, let him come: he that will, let him take the water of life freely."

4

THE SECOND DISCOURSE

(JEREMIAH 3:6)

Surely the time is short,
Endless the task and art,
To brighten for the ethereal court
A soiled earth-drudging heart:
But He, the dread Proclaimer of that hour,
Is pledged to thee in Love, as to thy foes in Power.

Keble

WE do not know how Jeremiah's first address was received. It was impossible for Jerusalem to have heard the eager pleadings of the young preacher, protesting so earnestly against the policy of its priests, without becoming aware that a new force had entered the arena of its public life. And from that moment, through the forty-four years that followed, the influence of his holy example and fervent words was destined to make itself mightily felt. One more star of hope shone over that hotbed of corruption, the very atmosphere of which was charged with symptoms of impending dissolution. Another voice was audible through which God could utter his pleadings and remonstrances.

In his second discourse, lasting from the third to the sixth chapters inclusive—and which perhaps is preserved as a specimen of Jeremiah's words at this period—there is an added power and pathos. The flame burns higher, the sword has a keener edge, yet the tone is more tremulous and tender. There is more than ever the spirit of Jesus, bewailing the blindness and obstinacy of men, as the vision of impending judgment looms clearer before the soul and the violence done to the redeeming love of God is more clearly apprehended. In his own touching words, Jeremiah was as a gentle lamb led to the slaughter (11:19); but he was also strong as a lion in the vehemence with which he strove to avert the doom already gathering on the horizon and threatening to devastate his beloved fatherland. If any pure and holy soul could have saved Judah by its pleadings, tears, and warnings, Jeremiah would have done it.

But it was not to be. The poisonous weed had struck its roots too deeply; the ulcer was too inveterate. The evil that Manasseh had sown had too thickly impregnated the soil. However, this did not appear in those early days of Jeremiah's ministry and, with all the hopefulness of youth, he thought that he might yet avert the disaster. Surely a voice warning of the rocks that lay directly in the vessel's course, and a firm hand on the tiler, might yet steer the good ship into calm, deep water!

This discourse is occupied with a clear prevision of the Chaldean invasion, with plaintive expressions of pity and pain, and with eloquent assertions of the redeeming grace of God.

1. THE PROPHET'S PREVISION OF APPROACHING JUDGMENT. At the opening of Jeremiah's ministry, as we have seen, the land was rejoicing in a brief parenthesis of peace, like a glint of light on a mountainside in a cloudy and dark day. It was a welcome contrast to the experience of the previous centuries. And it appeared probable that it might last. The mighty empire of Assyria was weakened by internal dissension; Babylon was becoming a formidable rival of

Nineveh; the Medes, under Cyaxares, were beginning to descend the western slopes of the Taurus; while in Egypt Psammetichus was too deeply engaged in expelling the Assyrian garrisons, consolidating his kingdom and founding his dynasty, to have leisure or desire to interfere with the tiny neighboring kingdom.

Thus Josiah was able to pursue his reforms in peace, and there was no war cloud on the horizon. It was on one of these days of Josiah the king (3:6) that the newly appointed prophet startled the men of Jerusalem and Judah as he made known what he had seen from his watchtower.

He had heard the trumpet summoning the peasantry from the open country to the fenced cities, leaving their crops at the mercy of the invader, to save their lives. He had descried the lion stealing up from his lair in the thicket to destroy the nations. He had caught the cries of the watchers from the northern heights of Dan to Ephraim, and so to Jerusalem, as they announced the advent of the invader. He had beheld the desolation of the land, the hurried retreat of the defenders of the holy city herself, some to thickets and others to holes in the jagged rocks. Yes, and he had seen the daughter of Zion gasping in the extreme of her anguish and crying, "Woe is me now!"

So real was the whole scene to him that we find him turning to his brother Benjamites, who had fled for shelter to the metropolis, bidding them flee still further south. He beholds the preparations for the siege and the chagrin of her assailants that the evening shadows of declining day interpose between them and her inevitable capture. He describes the invader as a mighty and ancient nation, gleaning Israel as men gather the last grapes into their basket—cruel and merciless as evening wolves. Their quiver a sepulchre; their sword a terror; their charging cry hoarse and deafening as the roar of the sea; their chariots and cavalry irresistible. The mere reports of their deeds were sufficient to induce in each hearer, as it were, the pangs of travail (1:15; 4:6–7,16,19; 6:9,19, 21). And the words of the young prophet were as fire to wood (5:14).

It has been supposed that these words referred to the invasion of the Scythians, who about this time poured in countless hordes over Western Asia. The cities of Nineveh and Babylon alone, because of their great strength, escaped; the open country was swept utterly bare; all who could not escape were barbarously massacred or carried off as slaves; villages and towns were turned into charred and smoking ruins. But these barbarian hordes do not fulfill the entire scope of the prophet's words. They do not appear to have entered Palestine but to have passed down on the eastern or western frontier, skirting the territory of Josiah and driving the panic-stricken people to the shelter of the larger cities—from which the path of the invader could be traced by conflagrations kindled on their ruthless march. It is better, therefore, to refer these ominous words to the invasion of Judah by Babylon, which was to take place in thirty years, but of which the people were amply warned, that they might put away their abominations and return to the Fountain of Living Waters.

2. HIS PLAINTIVE EXPRESSION OF PITY AND PAIN. The tender heart of Jeremiah was filled with the utmost sorrow at the heavy tidings he was called to announce. Throughout the book we constantly encounter the expressions of his anguish. True patriot as he was, it was hard for him to contemplate the impending destruction of the holy city. The noblest traditions of his people were represented in those cries which, for a little, demand our consideration.

"The sword," he says, "reaches to the soul." And again, "My heart! My heart! I writhe in pain! The walls of my heart will break! My heart groans within me; I cannot keep it still" (4:19, free translation). He identifies himself with his land, and it seems as though the curtains of his own tents are being spoiled, even in a moment. He struggles against uttering his message of judgment until he can no longer contain himself and becomes weary with holding in (6:11). He addresses Jerusalem as the daughter of his people and bids her gird herself with sackcloth and sit in ashes, mourning as for an only son (6:26). He asks how he may comfort himself against sorrow, because his heart faints within him (8:18). He wishes that his head were waters, and his eyes a fountain of tears, that he might weep day and night for the slain of the daughter of his people (9:1). He wanders alone over the mountains, weeping and wailing because the pasture lands are dry, because the lowing of the cattle and the song of the bird are hushed (9:10). "Woe is me!" he exclaims, "my wound is grievous."

He had no alternative but to announce the judgments which he saw upon their way; but there was a sob in the voice that predicted them. So far from desiring the evil day, very gladly would he have laid down his life to avert it. The chalice of his life was full of that spirit which led the Master in later years to weep as he beheld the guilty and doomed city. Many a great preacher of repentance in all the centuries of Church history has known something of this bewailing. Side by side with vehement denunciations of coming judgment, there has been the pitiful yearnings over lost men.

We need more of this. Nothing is so terrible as to utter God's threatenings against sin, which are predictions of its natural and inevitable outworking, with no sign of anguish or regret. If we are called to speak of judgment to come, it should be after hours of solitary prayer, weeping, and soul travail. It is only in proportion as we have felt for sinners that we can warn them. It is only in so far as we have known the Saviour's pity that we can dare to take up the woes he pronounced against Pharisee and Sadducee, or threaten the fate which he so clearly and awfully denounced.

Our mistake is in dealing with generals and not with particulars; or in using terms which have passed from hand to hand until their inscription is worn away. We have not realized the loss of one soul, nor the unutterable woe of hell for one apostate, nor the meaning of the undying worm and the unquenched flame. And probably the best way of entering into the meaning of any of these terrible conceptions is to try and realize what they would mean for any one soul who was dear to us as life. Then from the one we may pass to the many; from the one lost soul we may understand the meaning of a lost world. Let us look at these things from the standpoint of the Saviour, or of a parent's love, or of the soul itself; and when thoughts have saturated our hearts of the dishonor done to God, the loss sustained by Christ, the anguish wrought into the texture of one disobedient life—we shall be able to speak to men of the judgment to come, with streaming tears, tremulous voice, and breaking heart. Such preaching will always be a convincing and irresistible argument to turn sinners from the error of their ways. Nothing is more awful than to speak of the great mysteries of life and death, of heaven and hell, of the right and left of the Throne, without that compassion of heart which is borrowed from close communion with the Saviour of the world.

3. HIS ASSERTION OF REDEEMING GRACE. Few of the sacred writers have had truer or deeper views of the love of God. It is to the earlier chapters of Jeremiah that backsliders must always turn for comfort and assurance of abundant pardon. The word *backslide* is characteristic of this prophet.

To Jeremiah's thought, sin could not quench God's love. It may come in between man and wife, severing the marriage tie and leading the husband to divorce her whom he had taken to be his other self; but though our sin be more inveterate and repeated than woman ever perpetrated against man, or man against woman, it cannot cut off that love which is from everlasting to everlasting. The clouds may dim, but they cannot extinguish the sun. Sin may hide the manifestation of the love of God, but can never make God abandon his love to us (Jer. 3:1).

The love of God goes forth in forgiving mercy. He only asks that the people should acknowledge their iniquity, and confess to having perverted their way and forgotten their God. It were enough that they should accept the terms of the confession which he himself suggested: "Behold we come unto thee, for thou art the Lord our God"; and he assures them that though their sin and iniquity were sought for, there should be none (4:1; 50:20).

The love of God does not deal with us after our sins. He gives showers immediately on repentance. He does not keep his anger forever. He intervenes between us and trouble, as the soft sand between the homes of men and the yeasty foaming ocean. He waits to receive us back, saying, "If thou wilt return, O Israel, unto me, thou shalt return." Ours may be the pleasant land, ours the goodly heritage, ours the rest for the soul—all of which we had forfeited, but all of which are restored to us when we return.

What true and delightful conceptions of the love of God were vouchsafed to the young prophet! Many similarities between his expressions and those of Deuteronomy suggest that it was his favorite book—as, if we may venture to say so, it was our Lord's; and perhaps it was from that ancient writing, then newly discovered, that he derived his inspiration. But, in any case, his living spirit had drunk deep draughts of the everlasting, forgiving, pitiful love of God, revealed and given to men in Jesus Christ our Lord. Oh, blessed love!—through which backsliding hearts may be admitted again to the inner circle, and have restored the years that the cankerworm has eaten.

5

AT THE TEMPLE GATES

(JEREMIAH 7:10)

Bewildered in its search, bewildered with the cry,
  "Lo here! lo there, the Church!" poor sad humanity
Through all the dust and heat turns back, with bleeding feet,
  By the weary road it came
Unto the simple thought, by the Great Master taught,
  And that remaineth still:
    Not he that repeateth the Name,
    But he that doeth the will.

Longfellow

WE must read the records given in the Books of the Kings and Chronicles to understand the remarkable movement which was on foot during the time covered by the first twelve chapters of the Book of Jeremiah. In his collected words he scarcely refers to the great reforms being introduced by his friend, the king Josiah; and he is scarcely mentioned in the historical records. But there is no doubt that he was in constant and close communication with the king and the little group of earnest reformers that clustered round his person, and which included Shaphan, Hilkiah, the prophet Zephaniah, the prophetess Huldah, and his own friend, Baruch.

Josiah promoted measures of reform from the earliest

years of his reign; but at first he was opposed by the dead weight of national apathy to the cause he espoused. The worship of idols—for which there are twenty different terms in the Hebrew language—had so many fascinations from the use of the peoples around, and from its appeals to sensual passion, that the mass of the people had no desire to revert to the more austere and purer worship of their forefathers. Besides, had not Solomon the magnificent, four hundred years before, erected on the southern slopes of Olivet shrines to Ashtoreth, the goddess of Sidon, and to Chemosh and Milcom, the national gods of Moab and Ammon? The rites of heathen superstition were also maintained by a vast herd of false prophets and priests, who, like parasites, throve in the corruption of their time. There was a fatal compact and collusion between the two groups which boded no good for the efforts of the zealous band of reformers who gathered round the king, because they appeared to give a divine sanction to the abominations that were being perpetrated. A wonderful and horrible thing had come to pass in the land. The prophets prophesied falsely, the priests ruled at their direction, and the people loved to have it so.

The cooperation of Zephaniah and Jeremiah was therefore exceedingly valuable. While Josiah wrought from without, pursuing a career of uncompromising iconoclasm, they wrought from within, appealing to the conscience and heart—here pleading the claims of Jehovah on the thoughtless crowds, there taunting the idol worshipers with the futility of their reliance on the creations of their fancy, and again announcing the swift descent of national judgments on the national sins which were desolating the country.

But, notwithstanding their united efforts, the cause of reform moved slowly, or might even have come to a stand-still—as an express train when buried in an avalanche of soft snow—had not the discovery been made in the eighteenth year of Josiah's reign, giving a new and unexpected impetus to the ancient religion of Israel. And though it is not exactly an incident in the life of Jeremiah, he was so closely associated with the men who were principally concerned, and his third discourse is so evidently suggested by the reforms to which it led, that we must briefly touch on it.

1. THE FINDING OF THE LAW. At the time to which this incident must be referred, the Temple was under repair. It sadly needed it; for the lewd emblems of idolatry had been erected within its sacred precincts and, beside them, the dwellings of the wretched men and women associated with the impious rites permitted on the site where David worshiped and Solomon spread his hands in solemn dedicatory prayer. Probably also the fabric was showing signs of dilapidation and age, for two and a half centuries had elapsed since it had been completely restored by Joash.

The work was entrusted to the superintendence of Hilkiah, the high priest, who was assisted by a little group of Levites; and the cost was contributed by the people who passed through the Temple gates. On one occasion, the king sent Shaphan, his secretary and chancellor, who was the father of Gemariah and a good man—who afterwards defended Jeremiah (36:10–19, 25)—to take an account with Hilkiah of the money which had been gathered by the doorkeepers. When they had attended to this important business and delivered the money into the hands of the workmen that had the oversight of the work, Hilkiah, the high priest, informed Shaphan, the scribe, "I have found the book of the law in the house of the Lord."

It was a very startling discovery. The rabbinical tradition states that it was discovered inside a heap of stones, where it was hidden when Ahaz destroyed all the other copies of the holy books. Or it may have been hidden away in the Ark, which Ahaz may have removed to one of the side rooms of the Temple, where dust and lumber then concealed it. There has been much discussion as to what that roll of ancient manuscripts contained—some holding that it was the entire Pentateuch, others that it was the Book of Deuteronomy. It has even been asserted by some that a pious fraud was perpetrated on King Josiah and his contemporaries by some well-meaning individual who had just written the Book of Deuteronomy with his own hand, and now foisted it on Hilkiah and the rest as a venerable production dating from the days of Moses! To what miserable straits they are reduced who would have us accept such wanton speculations! Let the critics betake themselves to the examination of the ancient manuscripts, if they will. We thank them for the facts they bring to light; in their own province we give them credit for painstaking and erudition, but we refuse to accept their theories. Let them give us the facts and we can formulate the theories for ourselves. Even if it could be shown—which we hold it cannot—that Moses was not the author of the Book of Deuteronomy, it is surely utterly inconceivable that the mind through which that sublime treatise was given to the world could have been a party to a fraud so unblushing and scandalous as to palm off its own offspring under the august sanction of the name of Moses!

After careful thought, we are disposed to think that the Book of Deuteronomy is specially referred to here, though not to the exclusion of the other books of Moses. It seems unquestionable that this portion alone of the Pentateuch was ordained to be written out by each king on his accession and was read before the assembled congregation once in each seven years. The terms of the covenant made afterwards by Josiah and his people are precisely those with which the Book of Deuteronomy abounds; and the phrases which characterize it are perpetually recurring in the addresses and appeals of Jeremiah. This book dyed his speech, as it had done that of Amos, Hosea, Isaiah, and Micah.

Its discovery by Hilkiah made as great a sensation as that of the Latin Bible by Luther in the library of the old Augustine monastery at Erfurt. Shaphan read parts of it before the king, among them probably chapter 28. "And it came to pass, when the king had heard the words of the book of the law, that he rent his clothes." In hot haste he sent a deputation of his most trusted friends to one of the suburbs of the city, where the prophetess Huldah dwelt. Jeremiah may have been at this time at Anathoth; or he may have been too young in his work to be recognized as an authority in so grave a crisis. The question to be asked was whether the nation must expect to suffer all the awful curses which those words predicted; the answer was an uncompromising "Yes," though their infliction might be for a brief space postponed.

Forthwith the king summoned a mighty convocation of all the men of Judah, all the inhabitants of Jerusalem, the priests and the prophets, and the people, both small and great; from a platform erected in the entrance of the inner court, he read aloud all the words of the book of the covenant, which had been found in the house of the Lord. Further, he solemnly renewed the covenant between Jehovah and the people—that they would walk after the Lord, and keep his commandments, testimonies, and statutes. Perhaps, as one commentator suggests, an ox was slain and the king and people passed between the severed halves in witness of their solemn resolve.

Then the work of reform broke out afresh. The tide of popular feeling rose high, and the reformers took it at its flow. The black-robed priests were suppressed; the emblems of idolatry were cast out of the Temple, and burned outside the city; the dwellings of the miserable votaries of lust were destroyed, Tophet was defiled, and the high places leveled to the ground. Thus, outwardly at least, Israel became again true to its allegiance to the God of their fathers and free from the taint of idolatry.

2. THE DIVORCE BETWEEN RELIGION AND MORALITY. The

influence of the court, the finding and reading of the law, and splendid success of the great Passover which Josiah instituted—the glow of the crusade against the old idolatries—sufficed for a time to effect widespread reform. The fickle populace gave an outward adhesion, at least, to the service of Jehovah. The Temple courts were thronged; the rites and forms of the Levitical code were rigorously maintained; every point of ceremonial allegiance to the institutions of Moses was punctiliously observed. But there was no real change in disposition. The reformation was entirely superficial. Beneath the fair exterior the grossest forms of evil were seething in hideous corruption, now and again breaking forth into the light of day, but awaiting the death of Josiah, when they once more asserted themselves.

Jeremiah was profoundly disappointed at the result of a movement which had promised so much. He detected its true character and sought an opportunity of showing its insufficiency to avert the wrath of God—which was gathering like a thunder cloud upon the horizon. Taking up his position in the gate of the Temple, on the occasion of some great festival when the people of Judah were gathered with the citizens of Jerusalem to worship Jehovah, he poured forth a torrent of remonstrance and appeal.

He was not unaware of the attention paid by the nation to outward ritual, which they mistook for religion. The incense of Sheba, and the costly fine-scented cane fetched from Arabia or India and burned for the sake of its rich perfume, stole through the Temple precincts (6:20). They took care to speak of the Temple as the House of God and to stand before him as his people (7:10). The burnt offering and other sacrifices were rigorously distinguished from one another, the priests and people feeding on those parts alone permitted by the Mosaic ritual (7:21). It was the boast of the people that the law of the Lord had been committed to their charge and that they had therefore special claim upon his forbearance (8:8). And against every accusation which the prophet laid at the nation's door, they pointed to the order and beauty of the restored ritual, to their splendid Temple, to their privileged condition as the chosen of God—and cried, "The Temple of the Lord, the Temple of the Lord, the Temple of the Lord, are these!"

But alongside of this outward decorum, the grossest sins were permitted with unblushing shame. One of the charges which Jeremiah brings against his people is that they had lost the power of blushing (8:12). The shamefulness of their sin was apparent in their shamelessness. They oppressed the stranger, the fatherless, and the widow. Theft, murder and adultery showed themselves in open day. So frequent and atrocious were their crimes of violence that they seemed transformed into a horde of robbers—the Temple their den; lies flew from their tongues like arrows from a bow; and while men spoke peaceably to their neighbors in their ears, they were lying in wait to betray them. Though idolatry had been overthrown in the high places of the land, it lingered in the houses of the great, who squandered their silver and their gold, their blue and purple, on the wood which they had shaped into the fashion of a god.

There was an evident divorce between religion and morals; and whenever that comes into the life of a nation or an individual, it is fatal! Satan himself has no objection to a religion which consists in postures, and ceremonies, and rites. Indeed he fosters it; for the soul of man demands God and craves religion, and it is the art of the great enemy of souls to substitute the counterfeit for reality in order to quiet the religious appetite with the shows and effigies of the Eternal and Divine—much as a man might satisfy his hunger with food that lacked the elements of nutrition while his strength and vigor were slowly ebbing away. It can never be too strongly emphasized that the soul of man cannot rest or be content without God; but it is too apt to be cajoled with that which is not bread and which does not satisfy.

3. THE EXCUSES BENEATH WHICH THE SOUL OF MAN SHELTERS ITSELF.

(a) *Ritualism.* It was the old belief that God was bound to help a nation or person that steadfastly complied with the outward forms of religion, as if he had no alternative but to help his devoted worshiper. In one form or another this conception has appeared in every nation and age. "What more can God want," the heathen cries, "than that I should give burnt offerings and calves of a year old, thousands of rams, and ten thousands of rivers of oil; my first-born for my transgression, the fruit of my body for the sin of my soul?" "What more can God want?" cries the formalist of our time. "I was received into the visible church as soon as I was born; I have complied with all her regulations; I do my best to maintain her institutions and services; in all weathers I am present when her doors are open; and there is no demand made by her representatives to which I do not comply to the best of my ability. What lack I yet?"

The incessant remonstrance of the Bible is against such protestations—whether expressed or understood— as these. "What doth the Lord require of thee," says Micah, "but to do justly, and to love mercy, and to walk humbly with thy God?" (Micah 6:8). "To what purpose is the multitude of your sacrifices unto me?" saith the Lord, in one of Isaiah's earliest sentences; and he added, still speaking in the name of God, "Incense is an abomination to me." And here Jeremiah takes up the same strain. He says, in effect, "Put all your offerings together; abolish the sacerdotal distinctions which Moses bade you observe; relinquish all ritual; end festival and fast alike." These things are comparatively indifferent to God when sub- stituted for obedience and a holy walk (7:22).

Where the heart is right with God it will find fit and proper expression in the well-ordered worship of the sanctuary. It will find the outward ordinance a means of quickening the soul by the laws of association and expression; but the outward can never be a substitute for the inward. The soul must know God and worship him as a Spirit. There must be faith, repentance, and inward grace. "God is a Spirit, and they that worship him must worship him in spirit and in truth." Throughout the ages God has been seeking such to worship him.

(b) *Destiny.* Men often say, as the Jews did, "We are delivered to do all these abominations; we were made so. We are swept forward by an irresistible current which we cannot control" (7:10). How many a man lays the blame of his sin upon his Creator, alleging that it is only the outworking of the natural tendencies with which he was endowed! How many a woman has laid the blame of her unutterable fall upon the force of circumstances which held her in their grip! And there are some religious fatalists who have gone so far as to trace their sins to the elective decrees of the Almighty! Whatever truth there may be in the doctrine of predestination, it will not absolve you from sin in the sight of God and his angels. There is more than enough grace in God to counteract the drift of the current and the strength of passion.

(c) *Special privilege.* Many a soul has presumed on being a favorite of heaven. "I am wise; the law of the Lord is with me. He needs me for the preservation of his truth, the elaboration of his scheme. His cause is too deeply involved with me for him to allow me to be a castaway. I may do as I will and he will deliver." Ah, soul, beware! You are not indispensable to God. Before you were, he was well served; and if you fail him, he will call others to minister to him. See what God did to Shiloh (7:14) and to Jerusalem! How bare the site; how woeful the overthrow! "If God spared not the natural branches, take heed lest he also not spare you!" Take heed lest the kingdom of God be taken from you, and be given to a nation bringing forth the fruits thereof.

6

THE SOUL'S "AMEN"

(JEREMIAH 11:5)

Whatso it be, howso it be, Amen!
   Blessed it is, believing, not to see.
Now God knows all that is, and we shall then,
   Watso it be.
God's will is best for man whose will is free,
God's will is better for us, yea, than ten
   Desires whereof He holds and weighs the key.
                 Christina Rossetti

THE words of the prophet in chapter 11:5 are full of deep significance to every holy soul summoned to stand between God and other men. It has also far-reaching meaning for all who are passing through the divine discipline in this strange and difficult life. Jeremiah was conscious of the special current of divine energy which was passing into and through his soul. The word had come to him "from the Lord." This is one of three forms of expression that he employs. Sometimes, "the word of the Lord that came to Jeremiah"; sometimes, "thus saith the Lord"; sometimes, as here, "the word that came to Jeremiah from the Lord." Probably he felt that word as a burning fire shut up in his bones, which he could not contain. He must needs give vent to it; but when it has passed his lips, and he has time carefully to consider it, he answers the divine message by saying, "Amen, O Lord!"

There is something very sublime in this attitude. Jeremiah, as we have seen, was naturally gentle, yielding, and pitiful concerning the sins and sorrows of his people. Nothing was further from his heart than to "desire the evil day." Nothing would have given him greater pleasure than to have played the part of Isaiah in this decadent period of his people's history. But what was possible for the great evangelical prophet in the days of Hezekiah was impossible now. In Isaiah's case, the noblest traditions of the past, the patriotic pride of his people, and the promises of God—all pointed in the same direction. But for Jeremiah there was an inevitable divorce between the trend of popular feeling led by the false prophets and his clear conviction as to the word from God. It must indeed have been hard to prove that the prophets were wrong and he was right; they simply reiterated what Isaiah had said a hundred times. Why was the policy of resistance to the invader wrong when Jeremiah spoke while it had been right when Isaiah fired, with his own mighty faith, the entire people? In these earlier stages of his ministry especially, it must have been one long effort to stand by himself against the strong current of popular feeling and patriotism which colored the visions of the false prophets. And yet, as he utters the terrible curses and threatenings of divine justice and predicts the inevitable fate of his people, he is so possessed with the sense of the divine rectitude, so sure that God could not do differently, so convinced that, judged by the loftiest moral standards, the sins of Israel could not be otherwise dealt with—that his soul rises up; and though he must pronounce the doom of Israel, he is forced to answer and say, "Amen, O Lord!"

There is something like this in the history of the redeemed Church. When God has judged the woman that has corrupted the world with her fornication, and has avenged the blood of his servants at her hand—as the smoke of her destruction arises, the blessed spirits who had been learning the deepest lessons of divine love at the very source and fount of love are heard crying, "Amen. Hallelujah!"

In each of these cases it is extremely interesting to see how the sense of justly deserved and righteously incurred judgment corrects the verdict of mere compassionateness and enables the most sensitive and gentle souls to acquiesce in what otherwise had been resisted to the utmost.

Beside these two instances we may place a third in which our Lord, in the same breath as he appealed to the weary and heavy-laden to come to him, spoke of the mysteries which were hidden from the wise and prudent, but revealed to babes, and said, "Yea, Father; for so it was well-pleasing in thy sight." "Yea" is close akin to "Amen." "How many soever be the promises of God, in him is the yea: wherefore also through him is the Amen, unto the glory of God through us" (Matt. 11:26; 2 Cor. 1:20, R.V.).

This is also the utterance of the Holy Spirit. When the voice from heaven declares the blessedness of the dead that die in the Lord, "Yea, saith the Spirit." All through this dispensation the Holy Spirit is giving his affirmation to the utterances of the Church, and to the procedure of divine providence. Too deep for human ears to detect, the Spirit utters his "Amen."

1. THE SOUL'S AFFIRMATION.

(a) *In providence.* We often seem to be traveling through a difficult piece of mountainous country in company with a strong, wise, and gentle companion, who has undertaken to guide us to our destination. There are foaming torrents, black and hurrying, which we have to ford at the imminent risk of being carried off our feet; there are darksome woods and forests, where suns have seldom penetrated, and where wild beasts have their lair; there are paths paved with flints so sharp, and slabs of rock so slippery, that progress seems impossible, except at too great a cost; there are long stretches of dreary desert where the glare blinds, the sunbeams cut like swords, and the shadow of a tiny retem bush provides a grateful relief; there are steep hills, and paths so narrow that there is hardly room to pass along the ledge of rock while the dark precipice waits to engulf. In earlier days the soul started back horror-stricken; in later ones we pleaded for an easier, more pleasant path, and envied the lot of others; but now our life has become one long, deep and constantly repeated "Amen" to the choice of him who goes beside us, and in whose mind each step has been previously conceived.

Let us guard against mistake. It is not possible at first to say "Amen" in tones of triumph and ecstasy. Nay, the word is often choked with sobs that cannot be stifled and soaked with tears that cannot be repressed. So it was with Abraham when he tore himself from Ur of the Chaldees, when he waited weary years for his son, when he climbed with aching heart the steep of Moriah. And as these words are read by those who lie year after year on beds of constant pain, or by those who have lost the enjoyment of the presence of their twin-soul, or by those whose earthly life is tossed upon the sea of anxiety, over which billows of care and turmoil perpetually roll—it is not improbable that they will protest as to the possibility of saying "Amen" to God's providential dealings, or they will ask, Of what avail is it to utter with the lip a word against which the whole heart stands up in revolt? Is it not, it may be asked, an impiety, a hypocrisy, to say with the mouth a word that is so alien to the sentiments of the heart?

In reply, let all such remember that our blessed Lord in the garden was content to put his will upon the side of God—though his body was covered with the dew of anguish, pressed out from it as the juice of the grape by the tread of the husbandman! He did not chide himself. He knew it was enough if, in the lower parts of the earth to which his human nature had descended, he was able unflinchingly to affirm, "I delight to do thy will, O my God"; "not as I will, but as thou wilt!"

Dare to say "Amen" to God's providential dealings. Say it though heart and flesh fail; say it amid a storm of tumultuous feeling and a rain of tears; say it though it shall seem to be the last word that shall be spoken because life is ebbing so fast: and you will find that if the will doth acquiesce, the heart comes ultimately to choose. And as days pass, some incident, some turn in the road, some concurrence of unforeseen circumstances, will suddenly flash the conviction on the mind and reason that God's way was right, the wisest and the best. "What you know not now, you shall know hereafter," is the perpetual assurance of the Guide, and this is realized not in the world of the hereafter only but here and now, on the hither side of the Gate of Pearl.

(b) *In revelation* there are mysteries which baffle the clearest thinkers, the most profound theologians, the Johns and Pauls of the Church; paths that lose themselves in mere tracks on the moor; snatches of music and color which no mortal genius can work out; suggestions of movements in the spiritual world which defy the apprehension of the subtlest and greatest of the sons of men to follow. The man that tracks God's footsteps loses them in the depths; and the eye that pursues his workings is dazzled by a light above the brightness of the sun; and the argument breaks off with the cry, "Oh, the depth of the riches, both of the wisdom and knowledge of God! How unsearchable are his judgments, and his ways past finding out!" It must be so while God is God. We are partakers of his nature, as a child is of his father's. But the distance between our capacity of intelligence and the thoughts of God is not measured even by that between the dawn of a child's mind and the full splendor of his father's power—because this moves in the region of the finite, while that is a difference between the finite and the infinite. We cannot by searching find out God or know the Almighty. There is no fathoming line long enough, no parallax fine enough, no standard of mensuration, though the universe itself be taken as our unit, by which to measure God. High as heaven, what can one do? Deep as hell, what can one know?

But, though we cannot comprehend, we may affirm the thoughts of God. That we cannot understand is due to the immaturity of our faculties. We are in our nursery stage: our words are the babblings of infancy; our ideas the thoughts of a child. But we can accept, and admit, and acquiesce in, and affirm the things which eye could not see, nor the heart conceive, but which are revealed on the pages of Scripture.

There is no doubt that the death of Jesus Christ has fully met the demands of divine law; and though some phases of his atonement may at times perplex us, yet our soul confidently exclaims, "Amen, Lord!" We are ignorant of why God chose us, how Christ could combine in himself the nature of God and man, or in what manner the Holy Spirit regenerates the soul. "How can these things be?" is the question which often occurs to the devout student of revelation. But when God, who has come straight from the realms of eternal day, steadfastly affirms that which he knows, and bears witness to what he has seen, we receive his witness and say reverently, "Amen, Lord!"

(c) *In judgment.* God's judgments on the wicked are a great deep. The problems that encircle the question of present or future punishment are among the deepest and most awful that the mind of man can approach. Like Moses, we fear and quake when we climb the storm-girt sides of Sinai, and hear the pealing, thunderous curse, to be followed by the lightning flash of fiery indignation devouring the adversary. We may well turn aside from such considerations and ask if the time can ever come when we shall be able to consider with equanimity the awful suffering which they must incur who have rejected the love of God in Christ. Will heaven have any bliss to us so long as there is a hell? Will there be any possibility of happiness while one sheep is lost, one link absent in the bridal necklet, one stone deficient from the regalia, one voice missing in the chorus? A partial answer at least is given to these inquiries when we hear from the lips of the most gentle of the prophets, anticipating the destruction of his people, for which his eye was to trickle down with tears, "Amen, Lord!"

At present we cannot expect to attain too much of this condition of mind and heart, because our views of the divine rectitude are so imperfect, our estimate of sin is so slight, our knowledge of the conditions of the universe so inadequate. Did we know more of sin, of holiness, of the love of God, of the yearning pleadings of his Spirit with men, of the all-sufficiency of the measure he has taken for their arrest and salvation, of the barriers erected to stay the precipitate downward course of the wicked, we should probably understand better how Jeremiah was able to say, "Amen, Lord!"

There is a striking thought in Ezekiel 14:22–23 in which God says that when we see the way and the doings of sinners in the light that shall be flung upon their entire life-course from the great white throne, we shall be comforted concerning the evil that he shall have brought upon them. And the prophet goes on to show that God will make us know that he has not done in vain anything that he shall have done. That era has not yet broken, but it is a wonderful conception of the comfort and resignation which the added light of eternity shall bring into hearts perplexed and anxious as they consider the fate of the ungodly. Abraham shall be comforted over the destruction of the cities of the plain; Jeremiah shall be comforted as he reviews the fate of Jerusalem; and Paul shall be comforted as he considers the long alienation of the seed of Abraham from their land and their exile with wandering foot and terror-stricken heart in all the countries of the world. And we shall be comforted as we behold the destruction of the wicked.

2. THE GROUND OF THE SOUL'S PEACE. "Yea, Father!" It may seem at first sight as though it were impossible that the heart of man could ever be induced to acquiesce in the terrible and difficult matters touched upon in the previous paragraphs: as long as mothers love the sucking child and have compassion on their sons; as long as soul is wedded to soul by the strongest and most tenacious bonds of human love; as long as we can suffer, yearn, fear, hope, pity; while memory keeps the records of the past, and love reigns, and the mind holds her seat. It might seem the impossible dream of the imagination that what appears incompatible with the tender human feeling can be consistent with the love of God. "Surely," you cry, "there are things to which I never can assent, decisions I can never reaffirm, sentences I can never countersign, possibilities to which I can never say, 'Amen, Lord!'"

But does not this protest of the soul arise from the fact that you judged such things from the standpoint of pure emotion, or human reasoning, or perverted principles of human action; and that you need to stand in the sanctuary of God, which is the focus and metropolis to which the loftiest intelligences converge, in order to come in contact with the lofty morality and legislation of eternity? And do we not wrongly think that our love is more tender, our sympathy more delicate, our compassions deeper, than those of the Father?

When tried and perplexed with the troubles of life, turn from these, which will make the brain dizzy and the heart sick, and consider the Father of our Lord Jesus Christ, from whom every ray of love in the universe has emanated; and remember that nothing can be permitted or devised by God which is not consistent with the gentlest and truest dealings that an earthly father could mete out to the child of his right hand, his Benjamin, the darling of his old age. So shall you be able to say, "Amen, Lord!"

When face to face with the mysteries of the Atonement, of substitution and sacrifice, of predestination and election, of the unequal distribution of gospel light, be sure to turn to God as the Father of Light, in whom is no darkness, no shadow of unkindness, no note inconsistent with the music of perfect benevolence. He is your Father, the Father of our Lord Jesus Christ, the Father from whom every home life receives its tenderest touches. Dare to trust him; and in the strength of that trust to say, "Amen, Lord!"

When peering over the strong barrier of redemption that intervenes between you and the dark fate of the ungodly, when thoughts will force themselves upon the spirit as the cry of the insurgent mob might penetrate the sacred seclusion of a temple—look away from this and gaze into the face of the Father, which is turned in the same direction, and dare to believe that nothing can happen in heaven or earth or hell which is out of harmony with the love that has inspired parents towards their children; that breathed the love into Mary's heart as she clasped her babe to her bosom; or that yielded the Only-begotten to the horror of the cross for man's redemption: so there shall be a new tone in the voice of the soul that says, "Amen, Lord!"

In other words, we must not look into the dark and perplexing questions that seethe and boil like wreaths of vapor around us. We must look up to the blue sky of undimmed sunshine, our Father's heart. He must be love, beyond our tenderest, deepest, richest, conceptions of what love is. In his dealings with us, with all men, and especially with the lost ones, love is the very essence and law of his nature. Somehow, we repeat it, everything must be consistent with this all-persuasive nature and temper of the Divine Being; and in proportion as you dare to believe in the Father, you will be able to say *"Yes,"* which is a true rendering of the Greek word in our version translated "Even so" (Matt. 11:26).

3. THE TRIUMPH OF THE AFFIRMING SOUL. "Amen, Halle-lujah!" Jesus as he rested in his Father was able to say, not only, "Even so, Father," but, "I thank thee, Father." And so there shall come a day when the four-and-twenty elders, representing the redeemed Church, shall see the judgment of the great opponent of the Lamb's bride and say, "Amen, Hallelujah!"

Mark the addition of "Hallelujah" to the "Amen." Here the Amen and not often the Hallelujah; there the two—the assent and the consent, the acquiescence and the acclaim, the submission to the will of God and the triumphant outburst of praise and adoration. Let us anticipate that age when we shall know as we are known, and when we shall be perfectly satisfied, perfectly jubilant, perfectly blessed—when every shadow of misunder-standing and misapprehension shall be dispelled, and we shall join in the hymn of the redeemed Church: "Great and marvelous are thy works, O Lord God, the Almighty; righteous and true are thy ways, thou King of the Ages" (Rev. 15:3, R,V.).

7

THE SWELLING OF JORDAN

(JEREMIAH 12:5)

So they two went closer down
    To the River-side,
And stood in the heavy shadows,
    By the black, wild tide.

But when the feet of the Lord
    Were come to the waters dim,
They rose to stand, on either hand,
    And left a path for Him.

Ezekiel and other Poems

BETWEEN the incidents already described and the subject of the present chapter, a crushing calamity had befallen the kingdom of Judah. In the face of urgent remonstrances, addressed to him from all sides, Josiah, perhaps desirous of emulating the heroic faith of Hezekiah and Isaiah, led his little army down from the mountain strongholds to attack Pharaoh-Necho, who was marching up by the coast route to participate in the scramble for the spoils of Nineveh, then in her death throes. The two armies met at Megiddo, at the foot of Carmel, on the extreme border of the plain of Esdraelon, which has so often been a decisive battlefield. The issue was not long in suspense. Josiah's army was routed, and himself mortally wounded.

"Have me away, for I am sore wounded," said the dying monarch, and his servants bore him from his war chariot to another in reserve; but he died after a few miles drive, at Hadadrimmon. His death was the signal for such an outburst of grief throughout the land that it became in after-years the emblem of excessive sorrow. Zechariah could find no adequate expression for the anguish of Jerusalem when the people shall look on Christ whom they pierced and mourn, than that it should be like "the mourning of Hadadrimmon in the valley of Megiddon," when the land mourned, every family apart. It has been compared to the grief of Athens, when tidings came that Lysander had destroyed her fleet, and to that of Edinburgh on the evening of Flodden. Jeremiah composed an elegy on the death of his king and friend, which has not been preserved; and at once the fortunes of Judah were overcast with darkest gloom (2 Chron. 35:20–27; Zech. 12:11).

The next king, Josiah's son Jehoahaz, reigned but three months and then was led off with a ring in his nose, like some wild beast, to Egypt, where he died. Necho instituted his brother Jehoiakim in his stead as his nominee and tributary. But the four last kings of Judah reversed the policy of Josiah. They did evil in the sight of the Lord, and of Jehoiakim it is recorded that he wrought abomination (2 Chron. 36:1-8).

At the death of Josiah, the large party that favored idolatry again asserted itself. Of what use was a religion that had not saved its chief promoter from such a disaster? The reformation promoted by the good king had never struck its roots deeply in the land, and the vigor with which he had carried out his reforms now led to a corresponding reaction. The reformers fell under the popular hate, much as the Puritans did in the days of the Restoration; and Jeremiah especially came in for a large share of it. He had been the friend and adviser of the late king and had not scrupled to denounce, in the most scathing terms, the idolatry and licentiousness of his age. He had uttered terrible predictions of coming disaster, which were beginning to be fulfilled. Then arose the mutterings of a coming storm of hatred and murder. Unknown to him, his countrymen were devising plans against him, saying, "Let us destroy the tree with the fruit thereof, and let us cut him off from the land of the living, that his name may be no more remembered."

The symptoms of this rising storm were unlikely to reach him, because he had been commanded to itinerate among the cities of Judah, as well as the streets of Jerusalem; and he had probably started on a prolonged tour throughout the land, standing up in the principal market places, and announcing everywhere the inevitable retribution that must follow on the breach of the divine covenant (11:8). The result of that tour was profoundly disappointing. A conspiracy was found among the men of Judah and the inhabitants of Jerusalem. They turned back to the iniquities of their forefathers; each city had its tutelary deity, each street its altar to Baal. And the conviction was wrought into the prophet's heart that intercession itself was useless for a people so deeply and resolutely set on sin. They had sinned the sin unto death, for which prayer is in vain (11:14; 1 John 5:16).

Disappointed and heartsick, Jeremiah retired to his native place, Anathoth. He was unsuspicious of danger, as a gentle lamb led to the slaughter. Surely among his brethren, in the house of his father, he would be safe and able to find the sympathy and affection for which his sensitive heart hungered, but which evaded him everywhere else. It was not to be. In this also he was to be like the Lord Jesus—who came unto his own, but his own received him not, and led him to the brow of the hill on which their city was built, that they might cast him down headlong. There was treachery in the little village.

The sacred tie of kindred was too weak to restrain the outbreak of fanatic hate. The priestly houses had winced beneath the vehement denunciations of their young relative and could bear it no longer. A plot was therefore set on foot and, under the show of fair words, they conspired to take the prophet's life. He had not known of his danger but for divine illumination: "The Lord gave me knowledge of it, and I knew it; then thou shewedst me their doings" (11:18, R.V.).

Stunned with the sudden discovery, Jeremiah turned to God with remonstrance and appeal. Conscious of his own rectitude and the rectitude of God, he was for a moment caught in the outer circles of the whirlpool of questioning, which has ever agitated the minds of God's oppressed ones, concerning the unequal distribution of earthly lots. "Righteous art thou, O Lord, when I plead with thee. Yet would I reason the cause with thee: wherefore doth the way of the wicked prosper? Wherefore are all they at ease that deal very treacherously?"(11:20; 12:1, R.V.).

1. THE APPEAL OF THE MALIGNED AND PERSECUTED SOUL. (a) *He was conscious of his own integrity.* Without doubt, Jeremiah was profoundly conscious of his unworthiness. He must have had as deep a conviction of sinfulness as any of the great prophets and psalmists of Israel. None could have lived as close to God as he did without an overwhelming sense of uncleanness. What Job felt, and Moses, and David, and Isaiah, must have been constantly present to his consciousness also. But in respect to this special outburst of hatred, he knew of nothing for which to blame himself. He had not hastened from being a shepherd, nor desired the woeful day, nor taken pleasure in the disasters he announced, nor spoken in the heat of personal passion. The sins of the people had procured the evils he predicted; and he had only sought to warn the reckless mariners of the rocks that lay straight in their course.

When we are reviled and hated, we should carefully search our hearts to see if we have given any just cause to those that hate and persecute us. The only suffering which comes within the circle of Christ's beatitude is that which is inflicted falsely, wrongfully, and for his sake. The man who endures grief, suffering wrongfully, alone can claim to be following in the steps of the Master and to be offering a sacrifice which is acceptable to God. He only can count on God's delivering aid.

The bursting storm should lead the captain to see that there is peace among his crew and amity with the other ships of the fleet! We have no right to complain of the wrong doings of others unless we are sure that, so far as we are concerned, we have given no just cause. But if we have done so, there is no option but to agree with our adversary quickly, though it involve leaving our gift at the altar. Every moment of delay aggravates the case and increases the difficulty of reconciliation. The course of justice is so rapid—from the adversary to the judge, the judge to the officer, and the officer to prison (Matt. 5:22–25).

(b) *He was perplexed at the inequality of human lot.* Every word of good Asaph's complaint in Psalm 73 might have been appropriated by Jeremiah. He had never swerved from the narrow path of obedience; at all hazards he had dared to stand alone, bereft of the comforts and alleviations that come in the lot of men; he did not scruple to bare his heart toward God, knowing that, to the limit of his light, he had done his bidding. But he was hated, persecuted and threatened with death while the way of the wicked prospered, and they were at ease who dealt very treacherously. Surely it was in vain that he had cleansed his heart and washed his hands in innocency. It was too painful for him. His feet were almost gone, his steps had well nigh slipped.

It is the question of all ages—to be answered only by remembering that this world is upside down, that the course of nature has been disturbed by sin, that the prince of the power of the air is god of this world, and that the servants of righteousness fight, not against flesh and blood, but against principalities and powers, against the rulers of the darkness of this world, the wicked spirits in heavenly places.

(c) *He was anxious for God's character.* There is a touch of apparent vindictiveness in his cry. "Let me see thy vengeance on them; pull them out like sheep for the slaughter, and prepare them for the day of slaughter." We are disposed to contrast these words with those that Jesus breathed for his murderers from the cross and that Stephen uttered as the stones crashed in upon him; and we think that there is an alloy in the fine gold, a trace of dross in the saint.

It is possible to adopt the suggestion that the prophet was predicting the fate of these wicked men, or that he was the divine mouthpiece in this solemn pronouncement of coming doom. But a deeper and more correct conception of his words appears to be that he was concerned with the effect that would be produced on his people if Jehovah passed by the sin of his persecutors and intending murderers. It was as though the prophet feared lest his own undeserved sufferings might lead men to reason that wrongdoing was more likely to promote their prosperity than integrity and holiness. Josiah was the one God-fearing monarch of his time, but he was slain in battle; *he* was the devoted servant of God, and his life was one long agony: was it the best policy then to fear God? Might it not be wiser, safer, better, to worship the gods of the surrounding peoples, who seemed well able to defend their votaries, and to promote the prosperity of the great kingdoms that maintained their temples? As Jeremiah beheld the blasting influence of sin—how the land mourned, the herbs were withered and the beasts and birds consumed—his heart misgave him. He saw no limit to the awful evil of his times so long as God seemed indifferent to its prevalence. Therefore he cried for vengeance, not for the gratification of his own feeling but for the sake of Israel.

(d) *He also rolled his cause on God.* So might 11:20 be rendered: "On thee have I rolled my cause." Ah, this was wise! And it is our only safety in times of great soul-anguish. The Divine Sufferer did this on the cross. "When reviled, he reviled not again; but committed himself to him that judgeth righteously." In his steps we must plant our feet. When men malign and plot against us, when friends forsake, when difficulties like Atlantic breakers threaten to engulf us—we must roll our anxieties from ourselves upon the blessed Lord, our burden-bearer, and leave them with him. The care ceases to be ours when it has been committed to him. He will see to all for us with a love so strong and tender and true that we need have no further cause for fear. Roll yourself, your burden, and your way on the Lord.

2. THE DIVINE REPLY. God stooped over his life, and said: "Do you not remember when I first called you to be my prophet that I foreshadowed the loneliness and isolation, the difficulty and persecution, which were in store? Do you not remember that I told you that you would have to be a brazen wall against the whole people? Have you already lost heart? Are you so soon discouraged? Has the first brush of opposition mastered your heroic courage? You have as yet run with footmen; presently you will encounter horses: you are now in the land of comparative peace, your native village, where those surround you who have known you from your childhood, and yet you are dismayed; but how will you do when a tide of sorrow comes upon this land, as when the Jordan leaps its banks, swells over the low-lying land around, and drives the wild beasts from their lair—how then?"

Does not God ever deal with us thus? He does not put us at once to contend with horses, but tests us first with footmen. He does not allow any one of us with frail and fainting courage to meet the overflowing floods of Jordan; but he causes us first to be tested in our homestead—the land of peace, where we are comparatively secure amidst those who know and love us. God graduates the trials of our life; he allows the lesser to precede the greater. He gives us the opportunity of learning to trust him in slighter difficulties, that faith may become muscular and strong, and that we may be able to walk to him amid the surge of the ocean. Be sure that whatever your sorrows and troubles are at this hour, God has allowed them to come to afford you an opportunity of preparation for future days. Do not be discouraged, or give up the fight, or be unfaithful in the very little. Do not say you cannot bear it. You can!

There is sufficient grace in God; appropriate it, use it, rest upon him. Be very thankful that he has given you this time of discipline and of searching; and now, taking to yourself all that he waits to give—the grace, and comfort, and assurance—go forward! He cannot fail you. What he is in the lesser he will be much more in the greater. The grace he gives today is but as a silver thread compared to the river of grace he will give to you tomorrow. If you start back now, you will miss the greater discipline that will surely come; but in missing it you will also miss the greater revelation of himself that will accompany the discipline. Be true to God! Trust in God, and remember that when he brings you to the swelling of Jordan—not necessarily death, but some awful flood of sorrow—that then, for the first time perhaps, you will meet the ark and the Priest whose feet, when they dip in the margin of the river, will cause it to part, and you will go over dry-shod. When Jordan overflows its banks, God brings his chosen people to the brink, and it is then that he cleaves the path through the heart of the river, so that they are not touched by its descending torrent.

8

THE DROUGHT

(JEREMIAH 14-15)

If, in the paths of the world,
Stones might have wounded thy feet,
Toil or dejection have tried
Thy spirit—of that we saw
Nothing; to us thou wast still
Cheerful, and helpful, and firm;
Therefore to thee it was given
Many to save with thyself;
And at the end of thy day,
O faithful shepherd! to come,
Bringing thy sheep in thy hand.

Arnold

THE reign of Jehoiakim was still young. Necho was back in Egypt; Nineveh was tottering to her fall; Babylon was slowly growing upon the horizon as the rival of each great empire, and as the future desolator of Judah. Meanwhile, the chosen people, like a tree whose heart is eaten away with insects, was corrupted by innumerable evils. As a premonition of coming destruction, and as though the Almighty would make one last effort to arouse them to the awfulness and imminence of their peril, a terrible drought cast its sere mantle over the land. It had often been predicted among the other results of disobedience, but probably never before had it fallen with such desolating effect (Lev. 26:20; Deut. 11:17; 28:23).

The whole land was filled with mourning. In the places of public concourse, where the people gathered in the burning sunshine, they sat in black garments upon the hard ground. Accustomed to rely upon the natural resources of the country, nourished by the rivers and streams that gushed from valley and hill, they were reduced to the dire extremities of famine. The vines on the terraced hills were withered, the wheatfields were covered with stubble, and the pasture on the plains was yellow and scorched. The very dew seemed to have forsaken the land; where the river had poured its full tide, there were only a few trickling drops. The beds of the watercourses were filled with stones. And the bitter cry of Jerusalem ascended, made up of the mingled anguish of men, women, and children, whose parched lips might not be moistened.

The description given by the prophet is very striking. Want is felt in the great houses of the nobles, who send their servants for water without avail. The ploughmen sit in their barns with covered heads; it is useless to think of driving their ploughs through the chapped soil. The doe, whose maternal love has passed into a proverb, is represented as forsaking her young, that she may seek for grass. The wild asses stand on the bare heights and eagerly snuff up what breeze may pass over the land in the evening, to relieve the agony of the fever of their thirst. All the land bakes like an oven; and the sun, as he passes daily through a brazen sky, looks down on scenes of unutterable horror.

What a picture is this of the desolation that sometimes overtakes a Christian community! Every faithful worker could tell of periods when it has seemed as though the cloud and dew of divine blessing had forsaken the plot on which he was engaged. There are no tears of penitence, no sighs of contrition, no blessed visitations of the dew of the Holy Ghost, no fresh young shoots of piety, no joy in the Lord, no fruits of the Spirit. Ah, then, work is hard and difficult, and the soul of the worker faints and is discouraged. Blessed is that church which has not known this time of drought, and which has not experienced in the spiritual sphere the counterpart of the utter failure of moisture in the natural.

It is at such times that the lover of his fellows gathers himself together to deal with the Almighty. You can see him entering the secret place of the Most High, prepared to speak with God and, if possible, secure a mitigation of the reign of the brazen sky and a return of those times of blessing that can only come from the presence of the Lord. His face is set with a resolute purpose. Through the weary eyes the fire of a mighty resolution is burning. With his two hands he is prepared to come to close dealings with God, as Jacob when he made supplication with the angel. Let us draw near, and overhear the colloquy between Jeremiah and the Almighty. It may be that we shall discover arguments that we may take upon our own lips when days of drought are visiting the Church at large, or that sphere of work in which we are called specially to labor. It is thus that the soul discourses with God.

1. THE PLEADINGS OF THE INTERCEDING SOUL. "My God, I come into your presence to acknowledge my own sin, and especially the sins of my people. I stand before you as their priest, to confess the sins which have separated between you and them, incurring your divine displeasure, and closing the avenues of communion. Our iniquities testify against us, and our backslidings are many. Once you seemed to abide in our midst; your smile a perpetual summer; your presence one long stream of benediction; your grace like a river making glad your city. But of late your visits have been few and far between. You have tarried for a night, and been away again at dawn, and we sorely miss you. Once you were as a mighty man, our

Samson, whose arm sufficed to keep our enemies at bay; but for long you have seemed overcome by an unnatural stupor, by a paralysis that holds you like a vice. And yet you have not really changed; you are our Saviour; you are in the midst of us. We bear your name. Your honor is implicated in our lot. What you could not do for any merit of ours, do for the credit of your name; do for the sake of your Son; do for the maintenance of your cause upon earth. Leave us not, nor let that foreboding prediction of Ezekiel be realized, when he saw the glory of the Lord recede by stages from the holy place, until it stood outside the city walls" (see 14:7-9).

The answer of the Divine Spirit. There are times when God seems to speak thus to the soul—if we may dare put our impression of his words in our own phrase: "It is useless, my servant, to pray. My grace is infinite; my mercy endures forever; my fullness waits to pour forth its tides, to make the wilderness rejoice and blossom as the rose. I have no pleasure in the parched wilderness; I would that it were springs of water. I have no liking for the glowing sand; I would that it might become a pool. But so long as men cling to their sins, so long as they perpetrate abominations like those which Ezekiel saw when in the chambers of imagery he beheld the elders of Israel offering incense to creeping things and abominable beasts, it is impossible for me to cause rain or give showers. Beneath the appearance of religious worship and decorum, evils are breeding that separate between my people and myself, and hide my face from them. These must be dealt with. You must begin to search the chambers of their hearts with candles, to show my people their transgressions and the house of Israel their sins. Your work now is not that of the intercessor, but of the reformer; not yet to plead with Elijah upon the brow of Carmel but, like Elijah, to extirpate the lurking evil of the people, as when he dyed the waters of Kishon with the blood of Ahab's priests" (see 14:10-12).

2. THE LAMENTS OF THE TRUE SHEPHERD. "Ah, Lord God! True, too true, sadly too true, are your words. Your people deserve all that you have said. Their iniquities are alone accountable for their sorrows. But remember how falsely they have been taught. The land is full of those who hide your truth under a cloud of words. They say that the outward ritual suffices, however far the heart is from you. There is grievous fault, but surely it lies at the door of those who mislead the fickle, changeful crowd. Their mouths are lined with wool; they cry, 'Peace! Peace!' when there is none. The very remonstrances of conscience are scattered because the shepherds have failed in their high commission" (see 14:13).

The answer of the Divine Spirit. There are days in the history of the Christian when he is called to walk upon the mountains of vision, and he overhears the attendant shepherds, of whom Bunyan speaks, talking to each other and saying, "Shall we show these pilgrims some wonders?" Beneath their guidance he climbs to the top of the hill called Error, which is very steep on the further side. At the bottom lie several men all dashed to pieces by a fall from the top. "What does this mean?" is the obvious inquiry. "Have you not heard of Hymenaeus and Philetus," is the reply, "who erred concerning the faith, as to the resurrection of the body? These are they." So in our pleadings for men, we sometimes obtain a glimpse of the inevitableness of the divine judgments and the irreparableness of the injury that false teachers may do to their fellows. There is no fate so terrible as of those who have not only erred themselves, but have caused men to err; who have been a stumbling block in the way of one of God's little ones. Better be dumb and not able to speak than say words that may destroy the faith of childhood, or start questionings that may shatter by one fell blow the construction of years. It was in this strain that God replied to the prophet.

"The doom of the false prophets will be terrible. Their

fate will be the more awful because they have run without being sent, and prophesied without having seen a vision. There has been no divine impulse energizing their words. Position, bread and power have been the incentives of their office, but the people have loved to have it so. Their corrupt morals have produced a corrupt priesthood, and a crop of false prophets. The men of whom you complain are the product of their times. My people, enervated with sloth, luxury and conceit, would not endure the simple truth of the divine Word; and this evil band have been bred and nurtured in the stifling corruption of the age. Until, therefore, the people themselves have put away their sin and returned to me in penitence and consecration, they must be held guilty before my sight and suffer the outworking of their sin. 'I will pour their wickedness upon them.'" (see 14:14–16).

3. THE INTERCEDING SOUL. "Granted, great God, that you are just, and right—yet you can not utterly reject. Your smiting cannot be unto death. You must heal. You may cast away those with whom you have not entered into convenant relationship, or on whom your name has not been named, or among whom the throne of your glory has not been set up; but you cannot deal with us as with them. There is a tie between you and us which our sin cannot break. There are claims which we have on you as our Father which the far country wanderings of the prodigal cannot annul. There are interweavings of your character and prestige with our history which no stroke of your pen can dissolve. Remember the convenant; remember your promise to your Son; remember your bride, whom you cannot put away; remember that we have no help but in you; remember the word on which you have caused us to hope—therefore we will still wait upon you. We are not worthy to be called yours, but we claim the kiss, the robe, the fatted calf" (see 14:17–22).

The answer of the Divine Spirit. It is as though the Lord said, "I am wearied with repenting. I have tried every means of restraining them and turning them to better things—now by winnowing out the chaff, and again by bereavement and sorrow, and again by the swift destruction of the sword. They have appeared to amend, but the improvement was only superficial. Now my mind is thoroughly made up. My methods must be more drastic, my discipline more searching and thorough. I will turn my hand upon my people, thoroughly purge away their dross, and take away all their tin; and I will restore their judges as at the first, and their counselors as at the beginning. Thus I will answer your pleadings on their behalf. The destruction of the city, the decimation of the people by sword and famine, the awful sorrows of captivity shall act as purging fires, through which they shall pass to a new and blessed life. Nothing else can now avail. Because of my love for them I cannot spare them. The prayers of my holiest cannot alter my determination, since only thus can my eternal purpose of redemption be realized" (see 15:1–9).

4. THE CRY OF THE INTERCESSOR. Here the prophet falls into a muse, and as he foresees the misrepresentation of his motives, and the certain hate which his unfaltering prediction of coming doom must excite, he wishes that he had never been born. So does the heart of the man of God fail; and if, like Jeremiah's, it is highly strung and keenly sensitive, it becomes the prey of the deepest anguish: "Why, O God, did you make me so gentle and sympathetic; so naturally weak and yielding; so incapable of looking calmly on pain? Would not some stronger, rougher nature have done your bidding better? Even now, have you not some man of ruder make to whom you can entrust this mission? There are skins more impervious to the scorching heat than mine; may they not go into these flames? Why this stammering lip, this faltering heart, this thorn in my flesh?" (see 15:10).

The answer of the Divine Spirit. "I will strengthen you for your good." It is as if God said, "My grace is sufficient for you. I have summoned you, with all your weaknesses, to perform my will, because my strength is only perfected thus. I need a low platform for the exhibition of my great power. To those who have no might I impart strength; in those who have no wisdom I unfold my deepest thoughts. The broken reed furnishes the pillar of my Temple; smoking flax gives light to my beacon fires. Be content to be a threshold, over which the river passes; be satisfied to be a rod in my hand which shall achieve the deliverance of my people. O frail, weak soul, you are likeliest to be the channel and organ for the forthputting of my energy. Only yield yourself to me, and let me have my way through you, with you, in you; then you shall be as the northern iron and brass which man cannot break" (see 15:11–14).

5. THE RESPONSE OF THE SOUL. "O Lord, you know. Things that my dearest cannot guess, which I cannot utter, which I am slow to admit even to myself: the hope that trembles like the first flush of dawn, and the fear that paralyzes; the conflict; the broken ideals; the unfinished sentences; the songs without words. You know. You are my all. Your smile strengthens me against reproach. Your words bring rifts of joy and rejoicing in my saddest hours. Your presence banishes loneliness when I sit alone. And yet sometimes a dark foreboding comes that you will be to me as a deceitful brook, whose intermittent waters fail, which is dry when most its flow is needed. I know it cannot be, since you are faithful; and yet what could I do if, after having made me what I am, you should leave me to myself?" (see 15:15–18).

The answer of the Divine Spirit. "Renounce your forebodings," God seems to say. "Come back from the far country of your despondency. I would have you stand face-to-face with me without a shadow of a cloud. Wait before me. Consider not your frailty, but my might—not your foes, but my deliverances. Put from you that which is vile; expose yourself to my refining fires, that all your dross may be expurgated. Divest yourself of all that is inconsistent with your high calling. Then you shall be as my mouth; you shall stand amidst the surging crowd as a fenced brazen wall; you shall be impregnable against the assault of fear; in the darkest hours, when floods of ungodliness might make you afraid, and the fury of hell be hurled against you, I will be with you to save and deliver. You may have neither wife nor child; but I will be to you more than they. And I will deliver you out of the hand of the wicked, and redeem you out of the hand of the terrible" (see 15:19–21).

"This is the heritage of the servants of the Lord, and their righteousness is of me, saith the Lord" (Isa. 54:17).

9

ON THE POTTER'S WHEEL

(JEREMIAH 18:4)

He fixed thee mid this dance
Of plastic circumstance,
This present thou, forsooth, wouldst fain arrest:
Machinery just meant
To give thy soul its bent,
Try thee, and turn thee forth, sufficiently impressed.
                                                    R. Browning

ONE day, beneath the impulse of the Divine Spirit, Jeremiah went beyond the city precincts to the Valley of Hinnom, on the outskirts of Jerusalem where, in a little hut, he found a potter busily engaged at his handicraft. "Behold, he wrought work on the wheels." Amid the many improvements of the present day, the art of pottery remains almost as it was as many centuries before Christ as we live after.

As the prophet stood quietly beside the potter, he saw him take a piece of clay from the mass that lay beside his hand and, having kneaded it to rid it of the bubbles, place it on the wheel, rapidly revolving horizontally at the motion of his foot driving the treadle. From that moment his hands were at work, within and without, shaping the vessel with his deft touch—here widening, there leading it up into a more slender form, and again opening out the lip. So that from the shapeless clay there emerged a fair and beautiful vessel, fit for the Temple court or the royal palace. When it was nearly complete, and the next step would have been to remove it, to await the kiln, through a flaw in the material it fell into a shapeless ruin, some broken pieces upon the wheel, and others upon the floor of the house.

The prophet naturally expected that the potter would immediately take another piece of clay and produce in its yielding substance the ideal which had been so hopelessly marred under his hand. Instead of this, however, to his astonishment and keenly excited interest, the potter with scrupulous care gathered up the broken pieces of the clay, pressed them together as at the first, placed the clay again where it had lain before, and *made it again* into another vessel, as seemed good to the potter to make it. Perhaps this second vessel was not quite so fair as the first might have been; still, it was beautiful and useful. It was a memorial of the potter's patience and long-suffering, of his careful use of material, and of his power of repairing loss and making something out of failure and disappointment.

O vision of the long-suffering patience of God! O bright anticipation of God's redemptive work! O parable of remade characters, lives and hopes! To us, as to Jeremiah, the divine thought is flashed, "Cannot I do with you as this potter? saith the Lord. Behold, as the clay is in the potter's hand, so are ye in my hand, O house of Israel."

The purport of this vision seems to have been to give his people hope that even though they had marred God's fair ideal, yet a glorious and blessed future was within reach; and that if only they would yield themselves to the touch of the Great Potter, he would undo the results of years of disobedience which had marred and spoiled his fair purpose, and would make the chosen people a vessel unto honor, sanctified and meet for the Master's use.

The same thought may apply to us all. Who is there that is not conscious of having marred and resisted the touch of God's molding hands? Who is there that does not lament opportunities of saintliness which were lost through the stubbornness of the will and the hardness of the heart? Who is there that would not like to be made again as seems good to the Potter? "But now, O Lord, thou art our Father; we are the clay, and thou our Potter; and we all are the work of thy hand. Be not wroth very sore, O Lord, neither remember iniquity forever" (Isa. 64:8–9).

1. THE DIVINE MAKING OF MEN.

(a) *The Potter has an ideal.* Floating through his fancy there is the vessel that is to be. He already sees it hidden in the shapeless clay, waiting for his call to evoke. His hands achieve so far as they may the embodiment of the fair conception of his thought. Before the woman applies scissors to the silk, she has conceived the pattern of her dress; before the spade cleaves the sod, the architect has conceived the plan of the building to be erected there.

So of God in nature. The pattern of this round world and of her sister spheres lay in his creative thought before the first beam of light streamed across the abyss. All that exists embodies with more or less exactness the divine ideal—sin alone excepted. So of the mystical body of Christ, the Church, his bride. In his book all its members were written, which in continuance were fashioned when as yet there were none of them. So, also, of the possibilities of each human life. I know not if we shall ever be permitted, amid the archives of heaven, to see the transcript of God's original thought of what our life might have been had we only yielded ourselves to the hands that reach down from heaven molding men; but sure it is that God foreordained and predestinated us, each in his own measure and degree, to be conformed to the image of his Son.

See that mother bending over the cradle where her firstborn baby son lies sleeping! Mark that smile which goes and comes over her face, like a breath of wind on a calm summer's day! Why does she smile? Ah, she is dreaming, and in her dreams is building castles of the future eminence of this child—in the pulpit or the senate, in war or art. If only she might have her way, he should be foremost in happiness, renowned in the service of men. But no mother ever wished so much for her child as God for us, when first cradled at the foot of the cross.

To be like Christ, the type of perfect manhood; to be as much to Christ as he was to his Father; to reflect the face of Christ on men, as he the face of God; to fulfill the commission of redemption; to take up the cross; to be crucified with Christ; to rise and reign with him: all this is God's ideal.

(b) *The Potter achieves his purpose by means of the wheel.* In the discipline of human life this surely represents the revolution of daily circumstance; often monotonous, commonplace, trivial enough, and yet intending to effect, if it may, ends on which God has set his heart.

Many, on entering the life of full consecration and devotion, are eager to change the circumstances of their lives for those in which they suppose that they will more readily attain a fully developed character—hence, much of the restlessness and fever, the disappointment and willfulness of the early days of Christian experience. Such have yet to learn that out of myriads of circumstances God has chosen the lot of each as being specially adapted to develop the hidden qualities and idiosyncrasies of the soul he loves. Anything else than the life which you are called to live would fail in giving scope for the evolution of properties of your nature, which are known only to God, as the colors and fragrance which lie enfolded in some tropical seed. Believe that all has been ordered or permitted, because of that which lay entombed within you waiting for his call, "Come forth!"

Do not, therefore, seek to change, by some rash and willful act, the setting and environment of your life. Stay where you are until God as evidently calls you elsewhere as he has put you where you are. Abide for the present in the calling wherein you were called. Throw upon him the responsibility of indicating to you a change when it is necessary for your further development. In the meanwhile, look deep into the heart of every circumstance for its special message, lesson, or discipline. Upon the way in which you accept or reject these will depend the achievement or marring of the divine purpose.

You complain of the monotony of your life. "Day in, day out, the same round. Year after year, the same path trodden to and fro, no horizon, no space or width, only the same lane of sky between the high houses on either side. What scope is there here for the evolution of noble character? What opportunity to meditate and achieve great deeds?" Yet remember that the passive virtues are even dearer to God than the active ones. They take the longest to learn and are the last learned. They consist in patience, submission, endurance, long-suffering, persistence in well-doing. They need more courage and evince greater heroism than those qualities which the world admires most. But they can only be acquired in just that monotonous and narrow round of which many complain as offering so scant a chance of acquiring saintliness.

(c) *The bulk of the work is done by the Potter's fingers.* How delicate their touch! How fine their sensibility! It would almost seem as though they were endued with intellect instead of being the instruments by which the brain is executing its purpose. And, in the nurture of the soul, these represent the touch of the Spirit of God working in us to will and to do of his good pleasure. He is in us all, his one purpose being to infill us with himself, and to fulfill through us "all the good pleasure of his goodness, and every work of faith with power; that the name of our Lord Jesus may be glorified in us, and we in him."

But we are too busy, too absorbed in many things, to heed the gentle touch. Sometimes, when we are aware of it, we resent it, or stubbornly refuse to yield to it. Hence the necessity of setting apart a portion of every day, or a season in the course of the week, in which to seclude ourselves from every other influence and expose the entire range of our being to divine influences only.

The wheel and the hand worked together; often their motion was in opposite directions, but their object was one. So all things work together for good to them that love God. God's touch and voice give the meaning of his providences; and his providences enforce the lesson that his tender monitions might not be strong enough to teach. Whenever, therefore, you are in doubt as to the meaning of certain circumstances through which you are called to pass, and which are strange and inexplicable, be still; refrain from murmuring or repining; hush the many voices that would speak within; listen until there is borne in on your soul a persuasion of God's purpose; and let his Spirit within cooperate with the circumstance without. It is in the equal working of these two—the circumstance supplying the occasion for manifesting a certain grace, and the Holy Ghost supplying the grace to be manifested—that the spirit soars, as the bird by the even motion of its two wings.

2. GOD'S REMAKING OF MEN. "He made it again." The potter could not make what he might have wished; but he did his best with his materials. So God is ever trying to do his best for us. If we refuse the best, he gives the next best. If we will not be gold, we may be silver; and if not silver, there are still the earthen and the wood. How often he has to make us again!

He made Jacob again, when he met him at the Jabbok ford—finding him a supplanter and a cheat, but after a long wrestle, leaving him a prince with God. He made

Simon again, on the resurrection morning, when he found him somewhere near the open grave, the son of a dove—for so his old name Bar-jonas signifies—and left him Peter, the man of the rock, the apostle of Pentecost. He made Mark again, between his impulsive leaving of Paul and Barnabas, as though frightened by the first touch of seasickness, and the times when Peter spoke of him as his son, and Paul from the Mamertine prison described him as being profitable.

I have been told of a gifted son, who, when night has fallen and his old father has gone to the early couch of age, comes into the studio where the old man's hands had been busily engaged all day modeling clay, not without some fear that they are losing their skill, and removes all trace of senility or decay. So does God come to our work, when we have done our best and failed, and when men have turned from us with disappointment. He perfects that which concerns us, because his mercy endures forever, and he cannot forsake the work of his own hands.

Are you conscious of having marred God's early plan for yourself? His ideal of a life of earnest devotion to his cause has been so miserably lost sight of! Your career, as parent or child, as friend or Christian worker, has been such a failure! The grand chord struck in your early vows, at the marriage altar, or on the day of ordination, has been lost beyond recall; and the whole music has been so halting and feeble! For such, science and the competition of modern life have little encouragement. There seems no alternative but to go off into the rear and let others carry away the prizes that come so easily to them. While into the soul the conviction is burned: "I had my chance, and missed it; it will never come to me again. The survival of the fittest leaves no place for the unfit. They must be flung amid the waste which is ever accumulating around the furnaces of human life." It is here that the gospel comes in with its gentle words for the outcast and lost. The bruised reed is made again into a pillar for the Temple of God. The feebly smoking flax is kindled to a flame. The waste products are shown to be of extraordinary value, yielding the fairest colors, or providing the elementary principles of life.

3. OUR ATTITUDE TOWARDS THE GREAT POTTER. Yield to him! Each particle in the clay seems to say "Yes" to wheel and hand. And in proportion as this is the case, the work goes merrily on. If there be rebellion and resistance, the work of the potter is marred. Let God have his way with you. Let his will be done in you as in heaven. Bear it, even when you cannot do it. Be sure to say "Yes." There are times when we are not conscious that he is doing right. Life is often like the gray aspect of nature in February, when spring waits just outside the portal, longing to touch all things with her magic wand. It seems as if no one is concerned about "all the miles of unsprung wheat," or responsible for leaf or bud. Yet in myriads upon myriads of graves where seeds lie buried, God's angels are busily at work, rolling away stones, and ushering in the new heaven and the new earth of spring. So when we have once committed ourselves to God, we must believe that he does not lose a single moment but is ever hurrying forward the consummation of his ideal.

We cannot always understand his dealings, because we do not know what his purpose is. We fail to recognize the design, the position which we are being trained to fill, the ministry we are to exercise. What wonder, then, that we get puzzled and perplexed! We strive with our Maker, saying, What are you making? or, He has no hands. Yet surely it is enough to know our Guide, even if we do not know which point he is aiming for in the long chain of hills. He knows all the mountain passes and will take the easiest.

There is special comfort in these thoughts for the

middle-aged and old. Do not look regretfully back on the wasted springtime and summer, gone beyond recall; though it be autumn, there is yet chance for you to bear some fruit, under the care of the great Gardener. In all, he inspires hope. He can turn the battle from the gate; make the lost iron swim; replenish the empty pitchers with new good wine; restore the years the cankerworm has eaten; and make failures into victories. He who was able to transform the cross from a badge of shame into the sign of victory and glory must surely be able to take the most hopeless, disreputable, and abandoned lives, and make them bloom with flowers heavy with fragrance and full of blessed promise. Only let him have a free hand. Whatsoever he says, do it, or suffer it to be done. Seek forgiveness for the past, then restoration and remaking at his hand. Reckon on God and, according to your faith, it shall be done unto you.

When the clay has received its final shape from the potter's hands, it must be baked in the kiln to keep it; and even then its discipline is not complete, for whatever colors are laid on must be rendered permanent by fire. It is said that what is to become gold in the finished article is a smudge of dark liquid before the fire is applied, and that the first two or three applications of heat obliterate all trace of color, which has to be again and again renewed. So in God's dealings with his people. The molding Hand has no sooner finished its work than it plunges the clay into the fiery trial of pain or temptation. But let patience have her perfect work. Be still, and know that he is God. You shall be compensated when the Master counts you fair and meet for his use.

10

THE FIRE OF HOLY IMPULSE

(JEREMIAH 20:9)

There is a stay, and we are strong!
  Our Master is at hand
To cheer our solitary song
  And guide us to the strand! . . .
Or if for our unworthiness,
  Toil, prayer, and watching fail,
In disappointment Thou canst bless,
  So love at heart prevail!

Keble

JEREMIAH'S nature reminds us of the Aeolian harp, which is so sensitive to the passing breeze—now wailing with sorrow, now jubilant with song; so delicately strung, so sympathetic, so easily affected by every passing circumstance was the soul of the prophet. The whole book mirrors the changefulness of his mood as the ocean, the perpetual heavens outspread above it—now blue as the azure sky, and again dark with the brooding storm.

There are many indications of this in the chapters before us. For instance, there is the exclamation: "Cursed be the day wherein I was born; cursed be the man who brought tidings to my father, saying, A man child is born unto thee. . . . Wherefore was I born to see labor and sorrow?" (20:14–18). But in the same breath there is the heroic outburst, "The Lord is with me as a mighty one and a terrible; therefore my persecutors shall stumble, and shall not prevail" (20:11, R.V.). How great the contrast between these moods! In the first, he is traversing the valley of the shadow, where the dark trees shut out the sky, and the swollen torrent rushes turbidly through the gorge; in the second, he stands upon the heights where the sun shines and the landscape lies outspread to the far horizon, its wheatfields goldening in the summer sun.

The same contrast appears in this verse. There we find the half-formed resolution to make no further mention of God and to speak no more in his name. Then he is instantly aware of his inability to control the passionate outbursts of the Spirit within. "There is in mine heart as it were a burning fire shut up in my bones, and I am weary with forbearing, and I cannot contain" (20:9, R.V.). Oh, wonderful heart of man! Who can understand you? Who can estimate the heights to which you can rise or the depths to which you can sink? What an infinitude of bliss and of sorrow is within your compass! How radiant your heavens, how dark your abyss! It is well for us when we learn to distinguish between the life of our emotions and that of our will, and resolve to live no more in mood or emotion but to build the edifice of our life upon the granite of the obedient will.

1. THE CIRCUMSTANCES OUT OF WHICH THESE WORDS SPRANG. Jeremiah's half-formed resolution was "I will not make mention of him, nor speak any more in his name." Not improbably by this time Nineveh had fallen. For six hundred years she had ruled surrounding nations with a rod of iron tyranny, exerting an imperial sway with merciless cruelty. At last her time had come. A vast host gathered from Asia Minor as far as the shores of the Black Sea, from the entire valley of the Tigris, from Armenia, Media, and the wandering tribes

of the desert, and settled down on her as swarms of hornets on a putrid carcass. After a three-month siege the great city fell to a coalition of the Medes and Babylonians led by Nabopolassar, whose son, Nebuchadnezzar, was destined to be the "hammer of God." Rumors of this catastrophe were spreading through the world, carrying everywhere a sense of relief and foreboding—relief that the tyrant was down, foreboding as to who would take his place.

At this time Egypt was at the zenith of her power. Because of the decrepitude of Nineveh, Pharaoh had seized the opportunity of extending his empire to the banks of the Tigris. The kingdom of Judah, like all neighboring nations, owned, at least nominally, the king of Egypt as suzerain. Confidence in the proximity and prowess of his great ally encouraged Jehoiakim in his career of shameless idolatry and sin. The whole land, as we have seen, was corrupt.

Jeremiah, the foremost of the little band that remained true to the best traditions of the past, never lost an opportunity of lodging his complaint or striving to resist the downward progress of his people. In doing this, he aroused an ever-growing weight of opposition. The plot of his native town of Anathoth was the first volcanic outburst, to be followed by a long series of plots, and snares, and manifestations of hatred on the part of those for whom he would have gladly given his life as he daily gave his prayers. He sat alone, cast out by prophet and priest, by court and people.

"Come," they said on one occasion, "and let us devise devices against Jeremiah; for the law shall not perish from the priest, nor counsel from the wise, nor the word from the prophet" (18:18). He was a laughingstock all the day. Everyone mocked him. The word of the Lord was made to be a reproach to him and a cause for derision continually. His associates and those with whom he came in contact watched for him to stumble and whispered that perhaps he would be enticed, so that they could prevail against him and take their revenge on him.

Matters culminated finally in the episode of chapters 19 and 20. Under a divine impulse he procured a common earthen bottle and gathered together a number of the elders, leading them forth into the valley of Hinnom beside the gate of the potsherds. On this spot the refuse of the city was perpetually exposed to the foul birds and the wild dogs. It was a place of abhorring and loathsomeness. There he uttered a long and terrible indictment of the sins of his people, accompanying it with predictions of the certain and irrevocable doom to which they were hurrying. The men of Jerusalem would fall there by the sword before their enemies; in the confinement of the siege they would eat the flesh of their sons and daughters. The city itself would fall into ruins of blackened stones, and the surrounding valley be filled with the carcases of the slain making banquet for the fowls of the heaven and the beasts of the earth. To emphasize his words he broke the potter's vessel, pouring forth its contents in token that the blood of his countrymen would be shed to bedew and saturate the soil.

Not satisfied with this, he returned from Tophet and stood in the court of the Temple, perhaps on the steps that led up to the court of the priests. Crowds of people were engaged in some sacred rite; it may have been the time of one of the great feasts. When his voice was heard, a vast concourse must have gathered, whose angry faces and vehement gestures indicated the intensity of their dislike to the man who cast the shadow of impending destruction over their gayest hours. The endurance, of one of them at least, had at last reached its limit. Pashur, the chief governor of the Temple, to whose jurisdiction its order was entrusted, gathered a band of Levites, or Temple servants, seized the prophet, threw him on the pavement, scourged him after the Eastern fashion, and finally thrust him into the stocks, leaving him there the whole night, to the ridicule and hatred of the populace, to the cold night and the prowling dogs.

In the morning Pashur appeared to have repented of his harsh treatment; he released the prophet, whose strong spirit was not for a moment cowed by the indignity and torture to which he had been exposed. Turning on his persecutor, Jeremiah told him that he would live to be a terror to himself and all his friends. He then predicted that all Judah would be given into the hand of the king of Babylon, now mentioned for the first time; the people would be carried as captives to Babylon, and slain there with the sword; and all the riches and gains of the city, and all the precious things thereof, and all the treasures of the king of Judah, would be given into the hand of their enemies to carry to Babylon. And he declared that Pashur himself, with all his family, would be exiled to Babylon and would die there. It is this fourfold mention of Babylon that gives color to the suggestion that Nineveh had fallen. The strong hand of Nabopolassar and his son was beginning to show itself and to wield the sceptre which was falling from the faltering grasp of one of the oldest and greatest empires of antiquity.

Set free, Jeremiah went to his home and there poured forth that marvelous combination of heroic faith and wailing grief which is recorded for us that we may know the weakness of his nature and learn how earthen was the vessel in which God had placed his heavenly treasure. No brazen wall was he, but a reed shaken by the wind; no wise strong hero, but a child. What he did and said when face to face with his contemporaries was due to no native strength or heroism; as he says himself, his was "the soul of the needy" (v. 13, R.V.).

What a tale could be told by the walls of the secret chambers of God's greatest saints! What litanies of tears and sighs and broken sentences have beaten against them in successive billows of heart-rending sorrow! Take, for instance, that outburst of Luther on the eve of his appearance before the Diet of Worms. Those who have seemed strongest and most rocklike in the presence of their fellows have sunk most helplessly on the ground in solitude, confessing that none were so weak and helpless as they.

Our prophet seems to have gone even further. Then came a suggestion to his heart that he should relinquish his labors and renounce public for private life. Why struggle any more against the inevitable? Why set himself to convince those who would not be convinced and who repaid his love with hate? Why surrender name, comfort, and human love for the thankless task of endeavoring to stem his people's career? He came to the point of saying, "Send whom you will send; entrust your commission to some stronger soul, cast in a more heroic mold; let me go back to the seclusion and humble toils of my village home."

Not dissimilar have been the appeals of God's servants in every age, when they have measured their weakness against the strength of the evils they have combated and have marked their limited success: the handfuls of seed wasted upon barren soil; the word spoken in the ear of the wind; the futility of opposing an Ahab or a Jezebel; the ingratitude of those whom they would have gladly saved. They have been disposed to cry, with the greatest of the prophets, "It is enough, let me die!"

2. THE IRRESISTIBLE IMPULSE. "There is in my heart as it were a burning fire shut up in my bones, and I am weary with forbearing and cannot contain" (v. 9, R.V.) "O Lord, you are stronger than I, and have prevailed." Three things arrest us here.

(a) *The prophet's habit of turning from man to God.* Throughout the book there are so many indications of the close fellowship in which Jeremiah lived with Jehovah. God seemed always nigh at hand. His ear always bent down to the least whisper of his servant's need. Compelled to live much alone, this much-suffering man acquired the habit of counting on the companionship of God as one of the undoubted facts of his life. He poured into the ear of God every thought as it passed through his soul. He spread forth his roots by the river of God, which is full of water. There was no fear therefore that his leaf would become sere in the summer heat, or that he would cease from yielding fruit in the year of drought. The Lord was his strength, his stronghold, and his refuge in the day of affliction; and to God he opened his cause. "Heal me, O Lord, and I shall be healed; save me, and I shall be saved: for thou art my praise. . . . Let me not be dismayed or ashamed" (17:14–18).

Let us seek this attitude of soul which easily turns from man to God, not foregoing the hours of prolonged fellowship; in addition, let us acquire the habit of talking over our life with One who does not need to be informed of what transpires, but waits with infinite desire to receive the confidence of his children. Talk over each detail of your life with God, telling him all things and finding the myriad needs of the soul satisfied in him.

(b) *The burning fire.* We have sometimes seen a little steamer, like *The Maid of the Mist* at the foot of the Falls of Niagara, resisting and gaining upon a stormy torrent madly rushing past her. Slowly she has worked her way through the mad rush of waters, defying their attempt to bear her back, calmly and serenely pursuing her onward course, without being turned aside, or driven back, or dismayed. And why? Because a burning fire is shut up in her heart and her engines cannot stay, impelled in their strong and regular motion. Similarly, within Jeremiah's heart a fire had been lit from the heart of God and was kept aflame by the continual fuel heaped on it. Therefore, the difficulty with him was, not in speaking, but in keeping silent—not in acting, but in refraining.

This sheds some light upon the prophetic impulse, and helps us to understand what the Apostle Peter meant when he said, "Holy men of God spoke as they were moved by the Holy Ghost." It was as though the current of thought and feeling came mightily from without and, passing through them, swept them forward irresistibly. In this way it often happened that the prophets did not understand words which were put into their hearts by the Spirit of God, and of whose full meaning they were ignorant.

But, after all, our main desire is to know how we may have this heart on fire. We are tired of a cold heart toward God. We complain because of our sense of effort in Christian life and duty; we would gladly learn the secret of being so possessed by the Spirit and thought of God that we might not be daunted by opposition, nor abashed by fear. The source of the inward fire is the love of God, shed abroad by the Holy Ghost—not primarily our love to God, but our sense of his love to us. The coals of juniper that gave so fierce a heat to the heart of a Rutherford were brought from the altar of the heart of God. If we set ourselves with open face towards the cross—which, like a burning lens, focuses the love of God—and if, at the same time, we reckon upon the Holy Spirit—well called "the Spirit of Burning"—to do his usual office, we shall find the ice that cakes the surface of our heart dissolving in tears of penitence; and presently the sacred fire will begin to glow. Then the love of Christ will constrain us; whether we be beside ourselves, or be sober, will not be the subject of our consideration, but his Almighty Spirit, the thought of what he desires, the passion of fulfilling his will, shall destroy the fire of self-esteem and replace it with the sacred fire of passionate devotion.

When that love has once begun to burn within the soul and the baptism of fire has set us aglow, the sins and sorrows of men—their impieties and blasphemies, their disregard of God, of his service and of his day, their blind courting of danger, their dalliance with evil—will only incite in us a more ardent spirit. To see the multitudes rushing to destruction, to hear the boast of the blasphemer, the taunt of the infidel, the cry of the oppressed, the ribald mirth of the profane, the desecration of all that is holiest and best in man; to think of the grief caused to the Spirit of God, the dishonor done to him; to anticipate the outer darkness, the undying worm, the bottomless pit—surely, these will be enough to fan the smoldering embers of one's emotions into open flame, as when Jeremiah said that to restrain an inner impulse was a weariness, and to refrain from obeying it was a sin.

(c) *The prophet's safety.* "The Lord is with me as a mighty one and terrible; therefore my persecutors shall stumble, and they shall not prevail" (v. 11, R.V.). The presence of God is salvation. When Ezekiel describes the plot of Edom to take possession of the land of the chosen people, he indicates by a single phrase the futility of the attempt, saying significantly, "Whereas the Lord was there" (Ezek. 35:10). It was enough, though Israel was in exile, that God's Spirit was brooding over their desolate land.

Thus Jeremiah felt. He might be the weakest of the weak, having neither might, nor wisdom, nor power of speech, and apparently the easy prey of Pashur and Jehoiakim; but since God was with him, casting the mantle of his protection around his servant, and pledging himself to be Jeremiah's stronghold and house of defense, Jeremiah was invulnerable.

O weak and trembling soul, if you are true to God, God is with you, besetting you behind and before, and covering you with the shadow of his wing. You shall be like the city of the great King—the kings may assemble, but as soon as they see you they shall be stricken with terror and pass away; while you shall be a quiet habitation, a tent that shall not be removed, the stakes whereof shall never be plucked, neither shall any of the cords thereof be broken. "This God is our God for ever and ever; he will be our Guide even for evermore" (Psa. 48:14, R.V. marg.).

11

AFFLICTIONS, DISTRESSES, TUMULTS

(JEREMIAH 26)

I see the wrong that round me lies,
  I feel the guilt within;
I hear, with groan and travail-cries,
  The world confess its sin.

Yet in the maddening maze of things,
  And tossed by storm and flood,
To one fixed stake my spirit clings—
  I know that God is good.

                                    Whittier

JEHOIAKIM was, perhaps, the most despicable of the kings of Judah. Josephus says that he was unjust in disposition, an evil-doer, neither pious towards God nor just towards men. Something of this may have been due to the influence of his wife Nehushta, whose father, Elnathan, was an accomplice in the royal murder of Urijah. "Jehoiakim was twenty-five years old when he began to reign, and he reigned eleven years in Jerusalem; and he did that which was evil in the sight of the Lord his God." Such is the inspired epitaph by the chronicler.

Jeremiah appears to have been constantly in conflict with this king; and probably the earliest manifestation of the antagonism, that could not but subsist between two such men, occurred in connection with the building of Jehoiakim's palace. Though his kingdom was greatly impoverished with the heavy fine of many talents of silver and gold imposed by Pharaoh-Necho, after the defeat and death of Josiah, and though the times were dark with portents of approaching disaster, yet he began to rear a splendid palace for himself, with spacious chambers and large windows, floors of cedar and decorations of vermilion. As Elijah confronted Ahab, so did Jeremiah confront the young king with his terrible woes: "Woe unto him that buildeth his house by unrighteousness, and his chambers by injustice; that useth his neighbor's service without wages, and giveth him not his hire; . . . thine eyes and thine heart are not but for thy dishonest gain, and for oppression, and for violence." He further reminded him that the stability of Josiah's throne depended not on the splendor of his palace, but upon the justice with which he judged the cause of the poor and needy (22:13, etc.).

Clearly such a monarch must have entertained a mortal hatred towards the man who dared to raise his voice in denunciation of his crimes; and, like Herod with John the Baptist, he would not have scrupled to quench in blood the light that cast such strong condemnation upon his oppressive and cruel actions. An example of this had been recently afforded in the death of Urijah, who had uttered solemn words against Jerusalem and its inhabitants in the same way that Jeremiah had done. Such fury had been excited by his words that he had been obliged to flee to Egypt, from whence the king had secured his extradition, that he might avenge his bold denunciation by the sword and fling his body into the graves of the common people. Small shrift, then, could be expected by Jeremiah, if the king dared to take measures against him. But it would appear that this time, at least, his safety was secured by the interposition of influential friends among the aristocracy, one of whom was Ahikam the son of Shaphan (26:20–24).

1. THE DIVINE COMMISSION. Under the divine impulse,

Jeremiah went up to the court of the Lord's house and took his place on some great occasion when all the cities of Judah had poured their populations to worship there. Not one word was to be kept back. We are all more or less conscious of these inward impulses; and it often becomes a matter of considerable difficulty to distinguish whether they originate in the energy of our own nature or are the genuine outcome of the Spirit of Christ. It is only in the latter case that such service can be fruitful. And here for a moment we will turn aside to see how the heart of man may become the medium through which God can pour his thoughts on men, and the way by which we may recognize his inward prompting.

There is no greater enemy of the highest usefulness than the presence of the *flesh* in our activities. There is no department of life or service into which its subtle, deadly influence does not penetrate. We have to encounter it in our unregenerate life, when its passions reveal themselves, brooking no restraint. We meet it after we have entered upon the new life, striving against the Spirit and restraining his gracious energy. We are most baffled when we find it prompting to holy resolutions and efforts after a consecrated life. The Apostle Paul calls this the unequal marriage of the flesh, or self-life, with the holy law of God—a union which brings forth fruit unto death. And, lastly, it confronts us in Christian work because there is so much of it that in our quiet moments we are bound to trace to a desire for notoriety, to a passion to excel, and to the restlessness of a nature which evades questions in the deeper life by flinging itself into every avenue through which it may exert its activities.

There is only one solution to these difficulties. By the way of the cross and the grave we can alone become disentangled and discharged from the insidious domination of this evil principle, which is accursed by God and hurtful to holy living, as blight to the tender fruit. In the cross of Jesus, when he died in the likeness of sinful flesh, God wrote his curse upon every manifestation of selfish and fleshly energy; and now it remains for each of us to appropriate that cross, to accept the divine sentence, to lie in the grave where the voices of human ambition and adulation cannot follow us, to oppose the silence of death to the workings of our evil self. Not, however, to stay there, but to pass up by the grace of the Holy Ghost into the pure resurrection air and light where no face is visible but that of the risen Saviour, where no voice is audible save his, and where in the hush of perfect fellowship the spirit becomes able to discern the wish of its Lord.

2. THE MESSAGE AND ITS RECEPTION. There was a twofold appeal in the words Jeremiah was commissioned to deliver on this great occasion, when the whole land stood intent to hear. On the one side, by his lips, God entreated his people to repent and turn from their evil ways; on the other, he bade them know that their obduracy would compel him to make their great national shrine as complete a desolation as the site of Shiloh, which for five hundred years had been in ruins. It is impossible to realize the intensity of passion which such words evoked. They seemed to insinuate that Jehovah could not defend his own, or that their religion had become so heartless that he would not. Prophets and priests had assured the people that the very presence among them of Jehovah's Temple was a guarantee of their safety; and to suggest that a fate might overtake them like that which in the days of Samuel made the ears of every listener to tingle seemed the height of impertinence. "So it came to pass, when Jeremiah had made an end of speaking all that the Lord commanded him to speak unto all the people," that he found himself suddenly in the vortex of a whirlpool of popular excitement. Thus it befell Paul in later days, when the presumption that he had defiled the holy place produced so intense a paroxysm of popular feeling that all the city was moved, and the

people ran together, laid hold on him, and dragged him out of the Temple—so that he was with difficulty rescued by a regiment of Roman soldiers, who bore him by main force from the violence of the crowd, the multitude following and crying out, "Away with him!" (Acts 21:27-36). There is little doubt that Jeremiah would have met his death in a similar riot, had it not been for the prompt interposition of the princes.

Such is always the reception given on the part of man to the words of God. We may gravely question how far our words are God's when people accept them quietly and as a matter of course. The Word of God to those that hug their sin can only be as fire, a hammer and a sharp two-edged sword. And here again is a certain test whether our message is the product of our own fancy or the burden of the Lord. That which men approve and applaud may lack the King's seal and be the substitution on the part of the messenger of tidings which he deems more palatable, and therefore more likely to secure for himself a larger welcome.

3. WELCOME INTERPOSITION. The princes were seated in the palace, and instantly on receiving tidings of the outbreak, came up to the Temple. Their presence stilled the excitement and prevented the infuriated people from carrying out their designs upon the life of the defenseless prophet. They hastily constituted themselves into a court of appeal, before which prophet and people were summoned. The priests and prophets acted as the exponents of the people's wish and demanded sentence of death, turning from the court to the people to ask their concurrence. Then Jeremiah stood on his defense. His plea was that he could not but utter the words with which the Lord had sent him, and that he was only reaffirming the predictions of Micah in the days of Hezekiah. He acknowledged that he was in their hands, but he warned them that innocent blood would bring its own nemesis upon them all; and at the close of his address

he reaffirmed his certain embassage from Jehovah.

This bold and ingenuous defense seems to have turned the scale in his favor. The princes gave their verdict: "This man is not worthy of death, for he has spoken to us in the name of the Lord our God." And the fickle populace, swept hither and thither by the wind, appear to have passed over *en masse* to the same conclusion, so that princes and people stood confederate against the false prophets and priests. The conclusion thus gained was further confirmed by the voice of certain of the elders of the land, who had come from all the cities of Judah, and who reminded the people that the good king Hezekiah had acted very differently to the prophet Micah in listening to his remonstrances, entreating the favor of the Lord, and securing the reversal of the divine sentence.

Thus does God hide his faithful servants in the hollow of his hand. No weapon that is formed against them prospers. They are hidden in the secret of his pavilion from the strife of tongues.

Historical Connection

We have no narrative in Scripture of the fall of Nineveh except the prophecy by Nahum. "The Assyrian empire," says Dean Stanley, "vanished from the earth so suddenly, and so noiselessly, that its fall is only known to us through the reduced grandeur of the palaces of its latest king, and through the cry of exultation raised over its destruction by the Israelite prophet." Upon her ruins arose the Babylonian empire, first under the government of Nabopolassar, and afterwards of his greater son, Nebuchadnezzar. Ezekiel describes it as the rising of a mighty eagle, with great wings full of feathers of sundry colors, as though to indicate the variegated pennons of the various contingents that composed its vast hosts (Ezek. 17:3).

In a previous chapter we saw that Egypt was mistress of all lands from the Nile to the Euphrates. But as soon as the Chaldeans had established their kingdom upon the ruins of Nineveh, they turned their attention to wrest from Pharaoh-Necho some portion of his vast empire. Jeremiah had long before seen that this would be the case and had depicted, in graphic imagery, the scene and issue of the awful battle at Carchemish, by the Euphrates, where the two mighty peoples wrestled for the supreme power of the world.

He heard the call to arms. He beheld the horses heavily armed, and the horsemen with flashing spears and coats of mail. The Egyptian hosts, like the Nile at flood, pour themselves against the solid ranks of their foes; her tributaries from Cush and Put, together with the Ludim, famous at handling the bow, strive in vain to check the flight of Egypt's mighty men. They flee apace and look not back; the sword devours and drinks its fill of blood; the cry of the fugitive hosts fills the earth with clamor; and the mighty stumble, never to rise (46:1–12). Egypt never rallied again nor dared to do more than strive against the yoke that Nebuchadnezzar, with imperial might, fastened upon her.

After this there was nothing to stay the onset of Nebuchadnezzar, who probably had been associated in the kingdom with his aged father, and the first year of whose reign would therefore coincide with the fourth year of Jehoiakim (25:1). Like a leopard, to use the expression of Habakkuk, who at this time was beginning to exercise his ministry, the young king leaped upon the peoples that had been subject to Egypt and had aided in her expedition. And, as the tidings of his prowess spread through the world, Jeremiah foretold that he would be the scourge of God, to punish the abounding wickedness of the peoples. "I will send unto Nebuchadnezzar, the King of Babylon, my servant, and will bring him against this land, and against the inhabitants thereof, and against all these nations round about; and will utterly destroy them, and make them an astonishment, and an hissing, and perpetual desolations, and this whole land shall be a desolation and an astonishment; and these nations shall serve the king of Babylon seventy years."

In his first invasion of Judah, the king of Babylon contented himself with binding Jehoiakim in fetters to carry him to Babylon, though he seems afterwards to have changed his intention and to have restored him to his throne as his vassal, taking his oath of allegiance (Ezek. 17:12–13). He stripped the Temple of its precious vessels to enrich the house of his god at Babylon and carried into captivity several of the mighty of the land, among them Daniel and his three friends (Dan. 1:1–2). He then hastened back to Babylon, summoned thither by the tidings of the death of his father, Nabopolassar.

For three years Jehoiakim remained faithful to his oath (2 Kings 24:1); then he was deluded by the hope of independence, based on the hope of forming a confederation of neighboring peoples. Messengers went to and fro between himself and Pharaoh, negotiating for horses and much people, though all the while Ezekiel and Jeremiah protested that Jehovah would certainly punish him for violating his pledge to the king of Babylon. This was a time of unusual activity for the prophets of Jehovah, who strove their utmost to avert a political mistake, founded upon a moral obliquity, and sure to incur terrible vengeance (Ezek. 17:15–21).

It befell as they feared. Nebuchadnezzar, who was not prepared to brook such infidelity on the part of a subject king, soon put his forces in motion and prepared to advance across the desert to punish the weak and faithless Jehoiakim. It was during his march on Jerusalem that the incidents narrated in the two following chapters took place—the one the proclamation of a fast, the other the gathering of the Rechabites, with other fugitives, into the shelter of the city.

We have no certain clue to the prophet's history during these three or four years. His heart must have been filled with the patriot's anguish as he saw the coils of invasion drawn closer around the devoted city. To him, indeed, it was the year of drought, and there was no hope save in God; often upon his lips must have been words like those which the great Florentine* addressed to the city, which he loved with the passionate affection which the Jews always cherished towards Jerusalem, "Thy sins, O Florence, are the cause of these stripes. But now repent, offer prayers, become united. I have wearied myself all the days of my life to make known to thee the truths of the faith, and of holy living; and I have had nothing but tribulations, derision, and reproach."

* Girolamo Savonarola (1452–1498).

12

THE INDESTRUCTIBLE WORD

(JEREMIAH 36:23)

Truth, crushed to earth, shall rise again:
The eternal years of God are hers;
But error, vanquished, writhes in pain,
And dies amid her worshippers.

W E are admitted to the prophet's private chamber, where he is keeping close that he may not excite the acute animosity and hatred of the people. Baruch, his trusted friend, a man of rank and learning, sits writing with laborious care at the dictation of the prophet, whose soul is borne along by the impulse of the Divine Spirit. "Tell us," the princes said afterwards to Baruch, "how did you write all these words at his mouth?" Then Baruch answered them, "He pronounced all these words unto me with his mouth, and I wrote them with ink in the book."

When the scroll was filled, Jeremiah, not venturing to go into places of public concourse, entrusted it to Baruch and bade him read it to the assembled crowds. Jerusalem just then was unusually full. From all parts of Judah people had come to observe the great fast which had been proclaimed in view of the approach of the Babylonian army. Adopting the cry which Jeremiah had so fervently deprecated, "The Temple of the Lord, the Temple of the Lord are these," and imagining that there was a special virtue in the Temple precincts, the multitudes had crowded thither in an agony of fear, hoping by their black veils, covered lips, and heart-rending cries to propitiate the Almighty and avert the fate that seemed imminent.

Choosing a position in the upper court at the entry of the new gate to the Lord's house, Baruch commenced to read while the people stood densely massed around him. Amid the awestruck crowd was a young man, Micaiah, the grandson of Shaphan, who was so impressed and startled by what he heard that he hastened to acquaint the princes, then sitting in council in the chamber of the chief Secretary of State in the royal palace. They in turn were so aroused by what he told them that they sent him back to the Temple and asked Baruch to come without delay and read the prophet's words to them. He came at their request and, sitting among them, commenced to read.

In the group of princes were several notable men: Elishama, the Secretary of State; Elnathan, the father-in-law of the king, who had brought the prophet Urijah back from Egypt to die; and others. A great fear fell upon them as they heard those ominous words, which were probably closely similar to those recorded in the twenty-fifth chapter of this book. Though they had joined in the general hatred of the prophet, they were deeply sensible that there was everything to justify him in his prognostications of coming trouble; and it seemed their plain duty to acquaint the king with the contents of the scroll.

Before doing so, however, they counseled Baruch and Jeremiah to conceal themselves, for they well knew the despotic and passionate temper of Jehoiakim; and the scroll was left in the chamber of Elishama. It would appear that in the first instance they thought a verbal statement of the words they had heard would suffice.

This, however, would not satisfy the king, who bade Jehudi fetch the scroll itself. It was winter, the month of December; the king was occupying the winter quarters of his palace and a fire was burning brightly in the brazier. It is a vivid picture: the king was sitting before the fire; the princes standing around him; Jehudi reading the contents of the scroll; consternation and panic reigning throughout the city and darkening the faces of the prostrate crowds in the Temple courts. As Jehudi began to read, the royal brow knit and symptoms of a tempest of anger showed themselves. After the scribe had read three or four columns, Jehoiakim snatched the scroll from his hand and, demanding the penknife which he carried as symbol and implement of his calling, began to cut the manuscript in pieces, which he flung contemptuously into the fire. The worst have some compunctions, and for the most passionate there are warning voices that remonstrate and plead. Not so with King Jehoiakim. Delaiah, Gemariah, and even Elnathan, tried to dissuade him from his purpose, but in vain. Nothing could stop him until the whole scroll was cut to pieces and every fragment consumed. Not content with this flagrant act of defiance, he gave orders for the immediate arrest of Jeremiah and Baruch, an order which his emissaries attempted to execute, but in vain.

The destruction of the scroll did not however cancel the terrible doom to which the ship of state was hurrying, under the orders of its passionate and wicked captain. On another scroll all the words of the book which he had burned were written again; and others were added foretelling the indignity and insult to which the dead body of the king would be exposed. "His dead body shall be cast out in the day to the heat, and in the night to the frost."

1. EYES OPENED TO SEE. There was a vast difference between Baruch, whose heart was in perfect sympathy with Jeremiah, and Jehudi or the princes. But there was almost as much between the faithful scribe and the

heaven-illumined prophet. The one could only write as the words streamed from those burning lips; he saw nothing, he realized nothing; to him the walls of the chamber were the utmost bound of vision: while the other beheld the whole landscape of truth outspread before him, the rocks and shoals on the margin of the ocean, the inrolling storm-billows tipped with angry foam, the gathering clouds, the ship, straining in every timber, and driving sheer on the shore. For Jeremiah the walls of the chamber where they sat together were as though they had become transparent; he looked through and beyond them, and read off his message from what he saw, as a man might read from a book.

This was the work of the Spirit who inspired him, and whose special function it was to open the eye of the seers of the old time to the great facts of the unseen and eternal world, which were shortly to be reduplicated in the world of the temporal and visible. They beheld visions of God: the sapphire throne upborne by the strong cherubim; the terrible wheels of providence; the rise and fall of mighty empires; the subdual of sin and pain by the mighty sway of the coming One. To speak what he knew, and to testify what he had seen—such was the mission of the prophet.

In our case there is no likelihood of this. Yet men may be seers still. Two men may sit together side by side. The veil of sense may hang darkly before the one, while for the other it is rent in two from the top to the bottom. *There* no thought, no ambition, no desire for anything beyond the temporal and seen; but *here* the vision of the presence and care of God, of the principalities and powers in the heavenlies, of the ministry of angels and the opposition of fiends, of the chariots and horses of salvation, of the prize and crown, of the awards of Christ's judgment seat, and the home beyond the river. Flesh and blood do not reveal such things, but the Spirit of God. They are hidden from the wise and prudent but revealed to babes who love God. Happy are they, the eyes of whose heart are opened to know what is the hope of his calling, what the riches of his inheritance in the saints, and what the exceeding greatness of his power toward them that believe.

It is very important that all Christians should be alive to and possess this power of vision. It is deeper than intellectual, since it is spiritual; it is not the result of reasoning or learning, but of intuition; it cannot be acquired in the school of earthly science, but is the gift of him who alone can open the eyes of the blind and remove the films of earthliness that shut out the eternal and unseen. If you lack it, seek it at the hands of Jesus; be willing to do his will, and you shall know. It is a thousand pities to be blind and not able to see afar off when all around stand the mountains of God in solemn majesty; as the Alps around the Swiss hostelry, where the traveler arrives after nightfall, to eat and drink and sleep, unconscious of the proximity of so much loveliness. It is related of Ampere, the electrician, who was short-sighted without being aware of it, that when he became conscious of his defective vision through the casual use of the eyeglass of a friend, he burst into tears as he realized how much he had missed throughout his life of the wonderful beauty and interest of the world around him. With more reason will many of us have to lament our untold loss through that spiritual near-sightedness of which the Holy Ghost speaks (2 Pet. 1:9, R.V.).

If, on the other hand, you have the opened eye, you will not need books of evidences to establish to your satisfaction the truth of our holy religion, the glory of the risen Lord, the world of the unseen. With the men of Samaria, you will say, "We have seen it for ourselves." No further proof will be needed than your own spiritual senses afford. And though a series of well-ordered arguments should be brought into array to assail your position as a believer, you would be bold to reply, "Whereas I was blind, now I see." The patriarchs of old who reached forth their hands to greet the vision of the City that hath foundations, the New Jerusalem—which all holy souls behold descending out of heaven from God—furnish the model for spiritual men of every age; and they who see these things are indifferent to the privations of the tent-life, or, as in Jeremiah's case, rise superior to the hatred of man and the terrors of a siege.

2. THE USE OF THE PENKNIFE. Men use the knife to the Bible in varied ways. Among these are *Systems of Priestcraft and Error.* They have done it. They will do it again. They are wise to do it—I mean, wise in their own interests. For when once the Bible is in the hands of the people, the false teacher, who has deluded them for selfish purposes, must pack. The long reign of the Roman Catholic church began to break as Tyndale, Erasmus, and Luther opened the Word of God, and the printing press scattered it over the world. It is not to be wondered at therefore, that, to stay the progress of the Reformation as long as possible, fires were lit for Bible burning in every chief city of Europe, and the knife was freely used to cut out whatever condemned the office of the Pope, or the system to which he belonged. The Vulgate, with its mutilations and excisions, is a standing evidence that Jehudi's penknife survived his age.

The next that follows Jehoiakim's practice is *the Infidel,* who uses the keen blade of bitter sarcasm and miscalled reason to destroy the Scriptures. The hostility that manifested itself in the winter palace among the princes of this world has wrought in the halls of earthly learning and science, instigating similar acts to theirs. The laboratory of the chemist, the hammer of the mineralogist, the pry of the geologist, the telescope of the astronomer, the calculation of the arithmetician and the explorations of the discoverer—have all been used in turn as the penknife of destruction. The Bible is cut up regularly once in each generation by men like these.

The next are the *Higher Critics* of our time, who surely have gone beyond the necessities of the case in their ruthless use of the knife. Some of them seem to delight in making havoc of the sacred writings, hacking at the Old Testament especially, and whittling away from the reputed work of a Moses, an Isaiah, or a Daniel. There is room for the honest examination of the fabric of sacred Scripture, its language, the evidence furnished in its texture of the successive hands which have reedited its most ancient documents; but this is altogether different to the ruthless vandalism that wantonly assigns large portions of the Pentateuch to the age of Ezra, and the Book of Daniel to the times of the Maccabees.

We are all tempted to use Jehudi's penknife. It is probable that no one is free from the almost unconscious habit of evading or toning down certain passages which conflict with the doctrinal or ecclesiastical position in which we were reared, or which we have assumed.

In our private reading of the Scripture, we must beware of using the penknife. Whole books and tracts of truth are practically cut out of the Bible of some earnest Christians—passages referring to the Second Advent, with their summons to awake and gird on the armor of light; those that deal with the undying worm, the unquenched fire, and the inevitable doom of the ungodly; those that describe the types and shadows of the ancient law; or those that build up massive systems of truth and doctrine, as in the Epistles. But we can only eliminate these things at our peril. The Bible is like good wheat bread, which contains all the properties necessary to support life. And we cannot eliminate its starch or sugar, its nitrates or phosphates, without becoming enfeebled and unhealthy. It is a golden rule to read the Bible as a whole. Of course each will have his favorite passages, dark with tears and use—Psalm 23; Isaiah 53; John 14—but, beside these, there should be the loving and devout study of all Scripture, which is given by inspiration of God, and is therefore profitable, that the man of God may be perfect, thoroughly furnished to every good work.

3. THE INDESTRUCTIBLE WORD. Men may destroy the words and the fabric on which they are written, but not the Word itself. It is the incorruptible Word of God which lives and abides, though all flesh wither as grass, and the glory of man as the flower of the field. It must be sometimes an uncomfortable reflection to those who refuse the testimony of the Word of God, who to all intents and purposes destroy it and despise its remonstrances and warnings, that their attitude towards the message cannot affect the reality to which it bears witness.

Jeremiah wrote another scroll. The money spent in buying up copies of the Bible to burn at St. Paul's enabled Tyndale to reissue the Scriptures in a cheaper form and a better type. And perhaps the most remarkable fact in this connection is that, in spite of all that has been done to stamp out the Bible, it exists in millions of copies and is circulated among all the nations of the world—not a chapter effaced, not a parable dropped out, not a miracle injured, not a promise scarred. It has been declared over and over again to be a careless, unauthenticated collection of works of different periods, having no unity save that given by the bookbinder; yet it is with us today in unimpaired authority.

And the facts to which Jeremiah bore witness all came to pass. Neither knife nor fire could arrest the inevitable doom of the king, city, and people. The drunken captain may cut in pieces the chart that tells of the rocks in the vessel's course, and put in irons the sailor who calls his attention to it, but neither will avert the crash that must ensue unless the helm is turned. Let those beware who deny the testimony of Scripture to the retribution of sin and the wrath of God; these things are as true as the throne of God and the reward of the redeemed. You may tamper with and destroy the record, but the stubborn facts remain.

13

THE RECHABITES

(JEREMIAH 35)

Happy if full of days—but happier far
If, ere we yet discern life's evening star,
Sick of the service of a world that feeds
Its patient drudges with dry chaff and weeds,
We can escape from custom's idiot sway,
To serve the Sovereign we were born to obey.

Cowper

THE march of Nebuchadnezzar on Jerusalem was anticipated by incursions of Syrians, Moabites, and the children of Ammon. These days may be compared to the squadrons of light cavalry used in modern warfare to harass the enemy and prepare the way for heavier armaments. They swept up the valley, massacred the peasantry, devoured the crops, and spread terror on every hand. The inhabitants, therefore, of the neighboring country, eager to save their lives and some relics of their property, left their houses and lands to the mercy of the invader and fled for protection to the metropolis; accounting that within the massive walls of Zion they would find safeguard. What a stir there must have been as day by day the motley groups pressed in under the old gateways, gray with age, and sought accommodation and food in the already overcrowded tenements of the city!

Among the rest came a tribe that excited much curiosity by reason of its strange and antique manners. It came in full force—of men, at least. The sheik's name was Jaazaniah—"he whom Jehovah hears"; and his brethren and sons and the heads of other households were with him. They refused to shelter in the houses or permanent buildings of the city but pitched their dusky tents in some open space within the walls, and there awaited the turn of events.

Their record was an honorable one and reached far back into the early days of Hebrew history. When Israel was passing through the wilderness of Sinai, the tribe of the Kenites showed them kindness; this laid the foundation of perpetual friendliness between the two peoples. They seem to have adopted the religious convictions of Israel, and to have accompanied them into the Land of Promise. Retaining their integrity as a pastoral people, the Kenites maintained these friendly relations with Israel during the intervening centuries; and it was of this tribe that the Rechabites—for such was the name of this strange tent-loving people—had sprung (Judges 4:17–24; 1 Sam. 15:6; 1 Chron. 2:55).

About the time of Elijah, and perhaps largely influenced by him, the sheik, or leader of one branch of the Kenites, was Jonadab the son of Rechab. He was dismayed at the abounding corruption and iniquity of the time, and especially of the northern kingdom, then under the fatal spell of Jezebel's and Ahab's influence, which resembled some rank jungle in whose steamy air, heavy with fever and poison, noisome creatures swarm, and foul pestilences breed. In his endeavor to save his people from such a fate, this noble man, who afterwards became Jehu's confederate in extirpating idolatry, bound his people under a solemn pledge to drink no wine forever; neither to build houses, nor sow seed, nor plant vineyards, but to dwell in tents. Two hundred and fifty years had passed since then, but when they arrived in Jerusalem they were still true to the traditions of their race, and with sturdy strength stood out among the effeminate and idol-loving people of Jerusalem—living representatives of the noblest and purest days of Hebrew story.

1. JEREMIAH'S TEST OF THE RECHABITES. As soon as their arrival was noised abroad, and had come to the ears of Jeremiah, he was seized by a divine impulse to derive from them a striking object lesson for his own people. With an inventiveness which only passionate love could have suggested, the prophet caught at every incident and used every method to awaken his people to realize their true position in the sight of God. Taking the leaders of the Rechabites with him, he went into the Temple, to a room belonging to the sons of Hanan, known as a man of God, immediately adjacent to the room occupied by the princes and above that occupied by the gatekeeper.

Probably a little group of Jews, arrested by the prophet's association with these strange-looking men, followed them in to watch the proceedings. They were curious witnesses of the prophet's action, as he caused bowls of wine to be set before the tribesmen, and cups to be offered them, that they might dip them in and drink. They also heard the blunt unqualified refusal of these quaint, old-fashioned Puritans, "We will drink no wine," followed by an explanation of the solemn obligation laid on them centuries before.

The moral was obvious. Here were men loyal to the wish of their ancestor, though he was little more than a name to them, and refusing the offered sweets in which so many freely indulged. How great a contrast to the people of Jerusalem, who persistently disregarded the words of the living God perpetually remonstrating against their sins! The prohibitions of Jonadab were largely arbitrary and external; while those of Jehovah were corroborated by the convictions of conscience, and consonant with the deepest foundations of religion and morality. The voice of Jonadab was a cry coming faintly from far down the ages; while Jehovah was ever speaking with each new dawn, and in the voice of each fresh messenger whom he rose early to send.

There could be but one result. Judah, eaten through with the crimes and corruption against which God had protested in vain, must reap the whirlwind, as she had sown the wind. There could be no escape from the judgment which was drawing nearer with every daybreak. If the people could not heed words of expostulation, of entreaty and warning, accounting them exaggerated and vain, they should at least be compelled to admit that not one of God's threats of vengeance fell impotent on the air or missed its aim.

On the other hand, such devotion to principle; such persistent culture of simplicity, frugality, and abstinence; such literal adherence to the will of the father of their house—not only carried within them the assurance of perpetuity to the people who practiced them, but must receive the signature and countersign of the Almighty. "Therefore thus saith the Lord of hosts, the God of Israel, Jonadab, the son of Rechab, shall not want a man to stand before me for ever."

This phrase had a very profound significance. It suggested, of course, obviously, that the tribe would not cease to exist. And it is to be noted that Dr. Wolff, the missionary traveler, met a tribe in Arabia who claimed to be Rechabites, and read to them these words of Jeremiah from an Arabic Bible; and that Signor Pierotti, near the southeast end of the Dead Sea, met a tribe who also called themselves Rechabites, and quoted these words. But there was a yet deeper thought. The phrase is often used in Scripture of priestly service. And may we not infer that where we meet that devotion to principle and detachment from the world which characterized these men, there will always be a strong religious tone, a knowledge of God, a power in prayer and intercession, which are the essential characteristics of the priests? This will lead us to thoughts which are both suggestive and salutary.

2. THE ELEMENTS OF A STRONGLY RELIGIOUS LIFE. The phrase "to stand before God" designates a high-toned religious life, and includes the knowledge of God, the faculty of executing his commands, and the power of interceding for others. The phrase was a favorite one with Elijah, as expressing the spirit of his great career; and it was chosen by the angel Gabriel as conveying to the maiden of Nazareth the most certain guarantee of his authority and veracity. Surely, every reader of these words must desire that the spirit and attitude of all coming days may be designated thus. Oh to stand always before Christ, on whose face the glory of God shines as the sun in his strength! But if this is to be something more than a vague wish, an idle dream, three things should be remembered, suggested by the words of the Rechabites.

(a) *There must be close adhesion to great principles.* Many superficial reasons might have suggested to the Rechabites compliance with the prophet's tempting suggestion. The wine was before them; there was no sin against God in taking it; the people around had no scruples about it; and the prophet himself invited them. But against all, they stood on the principles which Jonadab had laid down to guide them; and they did not hesitate to avow them, let those ridicule who would.

In contrast to this, it is the general tendency among men to ask what is the practice of the majority; what is done by those in their rank and station; and what will be expected of them. We drift with the current. We allow our lives to be settled by our companions or our whims, our fancies or our tastes; and if ever we have a momentary qualm in contrasting our lives with the standards of primitive simplicity, of which Scripture and old biographies are full, we excuse ourselves by saying that so long as the main purpose is right the details are unimportant. This reasoning is wrong. We make a grave mistake in supposing that the main purpose of our life is something different from that which reveals itself in details. What we are in the details of our life, that we are really and essentially. The truest photographs are taken when we are unprepared for the operation. The true man, therefore, is always settling his life in its details, as well as in its main direction, according to great principles. Before we go another step, let me entreat my readers not to allow themselves to do or permit things simply because custom, or taste, or public opinion advocates them; but to bring their entire life to the touchstone of some elementary law of the kingdom of heaven which shall do in the moral what gravitation does in the physical sphere, ordaining the course of worlds and of molecules of dust.

And if it be asked, What principle is far-reaching enough in its scope, and powerful enough in its force, for so great a work? let us ponder what William Law so perpetually insists upon in his *Serious Call:* "The first and most fundamental principle of Christianity is an intention to please God in all our actions. It is because the generality of Christians have no such intention that they so fall short of true devotion." And, indeed, when we consider the characters of the early disciples of Jesus, or those of saints, martyrs, and confessors, must we not admit that they were as scrupulous in seeking the will of God about the trifles of their life as the Rechabites were in consulting the will and pleasure of the dead Jonadab? The thought of God was as present with the one as remembrance of Jonadab with the other. And was not this the secret of their strong and noble lives?

What a revolution would come to us all if it became the one fixed aim and ambition of our lives to do always those things that are pleasing in God's sight! It would not make us less tender in our friendships or less active in our service. It would not take the sparkle from the eye, the nerve from the grasp, or the warm glow from the heart. But it would check many a vain word, arrest many a silly jest, stop much selfish and vainglorious expenditure, and bring us back to whatsoever things are true, honorable, just, pure, lovely, and of good report.

(b) *Abstinence from the spirit of the age.* It was an immense gain in every way for the Rechabites to abstain from wine. Wine was closely associated with the luxury, corruption, and abominable revelries of the time (Isa. 28:1–8). Their abstinence was not only a protest against the evils which were honeycombing their age, but was a sure safeguard against participation in them.

In these days, the same principles apply. Whatever may be said about the use of alcohol for certain forms of sickness and debilitated health, it is incontrovertible that it is unnecessary as an article of ordinary diet. It is very closely identified with the vilest practices of impure passion, the obscenities of the music hall, the license of the stage, and the coarse revelry of the racecourse. Its fumes fill the card room, the billiard room, and the scene of abandoned vice. The votaries of sin confess that they could not do as they do, apart from its excitement. Add to all this the incontestable direct results of the drink traffic in crime, poverty, misery, suicide, and death—results which an eminent statesman once declared to be more deplorable than those that flow from famine, pestilence, and war combined. Surely, then, we shall do well to say with the Rechabites, whoever may ask us to drink, "We will drink no wine."

But wine may stand for the spirit of the age, its restlessness, its constant thirst for novelty, for amusement, for fascination; its feverish demand for the fresh play, the exciting novel, the rush of the season, the magnificent pageant. It is easier to abstain from alcohol than from this insidious spirit of our time, which is poured so freely into the air, as from the vial of some demon sorceress. We might well refer to this the wise words of the apostle: "Be not drunk with wine, wherein is excess, but be filled with the Spirit." You cannot exorcise Satan by a negation. You must be preoccupied, prepossessed. And it is only they that are filled by the Holy Spirit, in his blessed energy, who are proof against the intoxicating cup of this Circe world.

(c) *We must hold lightly to the things around.* The Rechabites dwelt in tents. They drove their vast flocks from place to place and were content with the simple life of the wandering shepherd. It was thus that the great patriarchs had lived before them (Heb. 11:9, 13). And ever since their days the tent-life has been the chosen emblem of the life that is so strongly attracted to the other world as to be lightly attached to this.

It is difficult to say what worldliness consists in. What would be worldly to some people is an ordinary part of life's circumstances to others. But all of us are sensible of ties that hold us to the earth. We may discover what they are by considering what we cling to; what we find it hard to let go, even into the hands of Christ; what we are always striving to augment; what we pride ourselves in. It may be name, fame, notoriety, pride of fashion, rank, money. But whatever it is, if it hinders us from living on the highest level—if it is a weight that impedes our speed heavenward—it should be laid deliberately on God's altar, that he may do with it as he will, and that we may be able, without frustration or hindrance, to be wholly for God.

14

HIDDEN BUT RADIANT

(JEREMIAH 36:26)

Be still and strong,
O Man, my Brother! hold thy sobbing breath,
And keep thy soul's large window pure from wrong!
That so, as life's appointment issueth,
Thy vision may be clear to watch along
The sunset consummation-lights of death!
E. B. Browning

AFTER Jehoiakim had deliberately cut in pieces the prophet's scroll, and so rejected his warnings and expostulations, and when in addition to this he had threatened the lives of God's faithful servants—it became clear that no further good could be gained by reiterating his messages. Thus the prophet's voice was hushed, apparently for the remainder of the reign of this bad and infatuated king. This is one of those principles of the divine government—which is as certain in its operation today as ever—that after a certain time the divine voice, being unheeded, ceases to speak; and those who will not retain God in their knowledge are given up to the workings of their corrupt minds, to work all uncleanness with greediness. We recall those ominous words, written as an epitaph on the grave of the first king of Israel: "Samuel came no more to see Saul until the day of his death," and the no less awful words of the apostle of love: "There is a sin unto death; not concerning this do I say that he should make request" (1 John 5:16, R.V.).

Into that new and splendid palace of Jehoiakim, whose spacious halls were ceiled with cedar from Lebanon, lighted by wide windows, and painted with bright colors, the one presence never entered which at that time would have saved the ship of state—as the timely arrival of a pilot may save an ocean steamer from the fatal ignorance of an incompetent captain. The false prophets might beguile the ears of king and people with predictions, bred in the falsehood of their own nature. The strong Egyptian partisans might urge on the king alliance with Pharoah as the certain cure for the difficulties of their position. But Jeremiah's voice, during the dark and troublesome days that succeeded that scene in the palace, and until Jehoiakim's body was cast forth, unburied and unwept, was still. How did it fare with the prophet, and what engaged him during those eventful years?

1. THE LORD HID HIM. What that precisely means it is impossible to say. Was there a John of Gaunt for this Wycliff, an Elector of Saxony for this Luther? Did Ahikam, who had before interposed on his behalf, or his sons—Gemariah, who loaned Jeremiah his room in the Temple for the reading of his scroll, and Gedaliah, who became governor of Judah after Zedekiah's deportation— take the prophet under their care? Or was this hiding something more divine and blessed still? In any case, whether through the intervention of second causes or directly, Jeremiah was hidden in the covert of the divine presence from the plottings of man and was kept secretly in a pavilion from the strife of tongues. In his first alarm he had said, "I am cut off from before thine eyes." Nevertheless, God had heard the voice of his supplication and had preserved his faithful servant.

These divine hidings are needed by us all. We must obey the voice that cries to us, as it did to Elijah, "Get

thee hence, and turn thee eastward, and hide thyself."
We are too prominent, too self-important, too conscious
of ourselves. Our shadows fall too much in front of us,
and we see them on the sand, clear-cut and defined. We
need to keep our faces sunward, that our shadow may
be well out of sight. And God must sometimes hide us in
the sick chamber, the valley of shadow, the cleft of the
rock. He calls us to Zarepath, or Carmel, to the privacy
of obscurity, or of solitude. It is only when self is hidden
in the darkness of the grave that the true light shines
upon our hearts, or the power of the true life emanates
from our acts.

How often has some timid nature sheltered and hidden
itself in a stronger personality to which it was devotedly
attached, so that it could bear, unmoved, the stare of
indifference, the affectation of superiority, the sarcastic
taunt, the injurious act! So when the one passion of our
nature is Godward, when his smile is our sufficient
reward, when we have no aim but to be well-pleasing in
his sight, we are hidden; and from our retreat in the
burning glory of his light, we can look out with equanimity
on the forms of dreaded evils as they pass us by.

There is a literal sense also, O tried and tempted
believer, in which God will hide you. It is stated that on
one occasion when the dragoons of Claverhouse were
scouring the mountains of Scotland in search of the
Covenanters, a little party of these godly folk, gathered
on the hillside for prayer, must have fallen into their
hands, had not a cloud suddenly settled down, effectually
concealing them from their pursuers. Thus the Son of
God still interposes for his own. Live to him alone. Be a
polished shaft, hidden in the hollow of his hand. Abide
in him. Hark! He says to you, as David to Abiathar,
"Abide with me; fear not! For he that seeks my life seeks
your life; for with me you shall be in safety."

2. HE REEDITED HIS PROPHECIES. To this period we may
refer the divine injunction: "Thus speaketh the Lord, the

God of Israel, saying, Write thee all the words that I have spoken unto thee in a book" (30:1–2). It may be that throughout this period Baruch continued to act as his faithful amanuensis and scribe. He, at least, was certainly included in the divine hidings (36:26–32). It was at great cost to his earthly prospects. He came of a good family, his brother being Seraiah, who held high office under king Zedekiah, and he cherished the ambition of distinguishing himself among his compeers. "He sought great things for himself." But he was reconciled to the lot of suffering and sorrow to which his close identification with Jeremiah led him, by a special revelation, assuring him of the speedy overthrow of the nation; and that, in the general chaos, he would escape with his life (45:5).

By the aid of this faithful friend, Jeremiah gathered together the prophecies which he had uttered on various occasions and put them in order, specially elaborating the predictions given in the fourth year of Jehoiakim against the surrounding nations. The word of the Lord came to him concerning the Philistines, and Moab, and the children of Ammon and Edom, Damascus and Kedar. And the devout student may well pause to read again the marvelous paragraphs, which foretell the fate of these nations beneath the all-desolating incursions of Nebuchadnezzar and his ruthless soldiers. "Thou art my battle-axe and weapons of war," said the prophet, addressing the great king in Jehovah's name; "with thee will I break in pieces the nations, and with thee will I destroy kingdoms" (see 47:1 to 49:33).

This time of Jeremiah's seclusion was therefore not lost to the world. It was fruitful as Bunyan's in Bedford Gaol, Luther's in the Wartburg, Madame Guyon's in the Bastille. Unseen, the prophet busied himself, as the night settled down on his country, in kindling the sure light of prophecy, that would cast its radiant beams over the dark waters of time until the day would dawn, and the day-star glimmer out in the eastern sky. Yield your whole nature to God, and be sure that he will bring all of it, and every moment, under his productive cultivation, so that it shall become like one of the old-fashioned wall-enclosed country gardens, every square inch of which yields some produce to the skillful hand of its owner.

3. HE MADE A DOUBLE JOURNEY TO BABYLON. To this period we must also refer the incident of the linen girdle or waistband, because the discourse founded on it was delivered during the three-month reign of Jehoiachin, which was altogether too brief to admit of so long a journey as was necessary for the purposes on which the prophet was set (see chapter 13, noting verse 18).

The Israelite was extremely particular as to cleanliness, and especially of linen. It therefore attracted universal notice that Jeremiah, at a certain period, wore a newly purchased linen waistband without washing it. When it was soiled and filthy, he took it, under divine direction, to the river Euphrates and there buried it in a hole of the rock. Some have thought that this is the description of a vision, or that some place nearer than the Euphrates, which was two hundred and fifty miles distant, is intended. But there seems no good reason for questioning the literal interpretation of the narrative, as given by the prophet. There was no special demand for his presence in Jerusalem, but the reverse. Time was no object in comparison with the vividness of the impression that would be produced. Besides, large purposes were served by his becoming familiarized with the condition of the exiles in Babylon, and with the drift of events there. In the prophecies which he delivered afterwards on the fall of Babylon, there are touches of description so minute and accurate as could hardly have been given by one who was not familiar with the city from personal observation.

After his return from Babylon, "many days" passed. Indeed, his second journey, to recover his marred waistband, may have been so timed by Almighty providence as to secure his absence from the city during the last scene of Jehoiakim's sad and tragic history, and to bring him thither again as Jehoiachin began his brief reign. But that rotted piece of linen, held up before the eyes of his people, told its own sad story. Judah and Jerusalem might have been to Jehovah for a name, a praise, and a glory, and God would have caused them to cleave to him; but they would not hear—they went after other gods, to serve and worship them. Therefore they were destined to be cast aside as worthless and unprofitable.

The lesson of this double journey, which must have meant about a thousand miles on foot, teaches us that no exertion on our part should be considered excessive if we can execute the commissions of our King. Long before, when a comparative child, Jeremiah had been summoned to perform God's errands for him (1:7); and it was not for him to complain if any special errand took him far afield, or involved journeying under scorching suns, and sleeping in the night dews. When Jesus bids us go into all the world, he means it; and we may not plead before him the distance and hardships of the way. It is enough if he has said, "Go to Euphrates." When once we are sure of this, we must imitate the prophet, who says, with charming simplicity, "So I went to Euphrates."

4. HE HAD VISIONS OF THE NEW COVENANT. There is much reason for supposing that it was in this time of seclusion that Jeremiah's eyes were opened to see a spiritual truth which was far in advance of any contemporary revelation, and was destined to become the mold into which some of the richest ore of gospel truth should be poured. It was not the last time when mortal eyes were closed in order to see; shielded from the glare of this world that they might behold the light that never shone on sea or shore. The *blind* Milton sang of Paradise lost and regained.

The exquisite poem to which we must now turn is

contained in chapters 30 and 31, and consists of some seven stanzas. The prophet is no longer concerned with Judah alone; his thought embraces the ten tribes also— "Israel" he calls them, or "Ephraim"—which one hundred and seventy years before had been carried away captive to Nineveh. But his heart exults as he anticipates the return of the entire people from the land of the north, baptized through suffering into a purer, nobler life.

On many of the exquisite thoughts and phrases of this joyful outburst, we might long and profitably dwell. We can only cull a few flowerets, and allow them to tell the wealth of the garden from which they come:

> Fear Thou not, O Jacob my servant, saith the Lord,
> Neither be dismayed, O Israel;
> For lo, I will save thee from afar,
> And thy seed from the land of their captivity.
>
> I will restore health unto thee,
> And I will heal thee of thy wounds, saith the Lord.
>
> Yea, I have loved thee with an everlasting love,
> Therefore, with loving kindness have I drawn thee.
> Again will I build thee,
> And thou shalt be built, O virgin of Israel;
> Thou shalt be adorned with thy tabrets,
> And shalt go forth in the dances of them that make merry.
>
> My people shall be satisfied with my goodness, saith the Lord.

Transported by words like these, as he lay in prophetic trance, it is not surprising that Jeremiah experienced, after a spiritual sort, the ecstatic joy which visits the soul when, between sleeping and waking, it realizes that its dearest hopes are being fulfilled. "Upon this I awaked and beheld; and my sleep was sweet unto me" (31:26).

But the more stupendous revelation was to follow. The dread commands of Moses, the elaborate forms of Temple ritual, the pleadings of Deuteronomy, enforced as they had been by the words of contemporary prophets, had all failed to withhold the people from backsliding. What hope was there that the distant future would not repeat the bitter story of the past? But God, who commanded the light to shine out of darkness, shined into his servant's heart and unveiled the glory of the new covenant, which was to be sealed by the blood of the cross—"the new testament in my blood," as Jesus called it. A covenant which would no longer depend on man's obedience to "Thou shalt," and "Thou shalt not"; but would glisten with the seven times repeated I WILL of God (31:31–34; Luke 22:20; Heb. 8:8–12).

That the law of God would not be *without* as a precept, but *within*, as though inwrought into the very structure of the heart and will; that religion would consist primarily in what God was to his child, rather than in what the child said or did towards him; that neither priest nor Levite would be needed any more, since each soul would possess the right of direct intercourse with its Lord; that sin would be completely forgiven, as if it had never been—this was the vision which shone in on the prophet's heart, and is realized in Christ for all who belong to him by faith. This blessed covenant shall yet gather Israel within its provisions.

It is a serious question how far that covenant has been fulfilled in our experience. We are enamored with the life it foreshadows, and sometimes we think that our inward parts and hearts do bear its sacred inscriptions, as did the stone slabs of Sinai the writing of the Decalogue. But we become suddenly conscious of some overwhelming irruption of covetousness, envy, pride and wrath—as though a sewer were to pour forth its filth over the mosaic work of some splendid pavement.

Such experiences stagger, but they should not discourage us. They probably show, not that God has not commenced his divine work, but that we have momentarily turned aside from him to make some effort of our own, or to pride ourselves on what has been accomplished.

Whenever God grants us a heavenly vision of some possibility in the divine life that beckons us from afar, as the stories of the world beyond the ocean stirred our sailors in the reign of Elizabeth, it is a positive sign that a time has come in our experience when God, who taught us to yearn for it, is prepared to realize it for us. Whenever Christ says, "I have appeared to you," he adds, "to make you." Our Father never discourages us by a promise which he is not prepared to fulfill; nor by a hope which he is not eager to bring to fruition. Let us turn back to God. Let us open our hearts and inward parts to his finger. Let us in meek humility wait for him to grave even more deeply and legibly his secret thoughts upon us. Let us believe that he is doing it. Let us reckon on him to perfect the inscription, and to keep it clear and clean.

Thus we shall know God. The dead past will bury its dead. The sins and iniquities of former days will be strewn on the shore like the corpses of the Egyptians from whom Israel had gotten free. And then our heart shall go out in the dance; our mourning will be turned into joy; our soul shall be as a watered garden; and God will comfort us, making us rejoice from our sorrow, and enabling us to reap in joy what we sowed in tears (31:10–14).

15

THE MINISTRY OF DESTRUCTION

(JEREMIAH 27–29)

Ours the shame to understand
  That the world prefers the lie;
That, with medicine in her hand,
  She will sink and choose to die!
Ours the agonizing sense,
  Of the heaven this earth might be,
If from their blank indifference,
  Men woke one hour and felt as we!

                                        Houghton

WHEN Jeremiah was first summoned to the work of prophet, it was summarized under six distinct divisions. He was set over nations and kingdoms to pluck up, and to break down, and to destroy, and to overthrow, as well as to build and to plant (1:10). Two-thirds of his work was therefore in the direction of destruction. It is not pleasant or easy work. No one would choose to stand amid the choking dust of some crumbling brickwork which is being pulled down to make way for a palatial structure to be erected on the site. Vested interests, long-established abuses, lucrative wrongs, cry out loudly against any attempt to interfere with their existence. But Elijah must precede Elisha; and John the Baptist must prepare the way for Christ. Before the seed sowing, the plough; before the outburst of spring, the stern disintegration of winter, rubbing the soil to powder in its mighty hands. Such was the work that fell to the lot of Jeremiah.

1. THE WORK OF DEMOLITION.

(a) *Jehoiakim.* When Josiah died, the whole land mourned. Each citizen felt personally bereaved, and appropriated the plaintive cries of professional mourners, saying, "Ah, my brother!" and "Ah, sister!" The air was full of the words. "Ah, Lord!" "Ah, the glory of Israel!" But Jeremiah foretold that at the death of Jehoiakim there would be no such expression. "He shall be buried with the burial of an ass, drawn and cast forth beyond the gates of Jerusalem." And again, somewhat later, when the king in impious defiance had burned the scroll, the prophet said, "He shall have none to sit upon the throne of David; and his dead body shall be cast out in the day to the heat, in the night to the frost" (22:13–19; 36:29–31).

The words of the prophet carried with them the imprimatur of Jehovah. They pronounced the inevitable sentence which God executed. And, therefore, though we have no certain record of the manner of it, it is more than probable that, on his return from his second journey to Babylon, Jeremiah received the tidings of the death of his inveterate foe. There are several traditions as to his death—one, that he was assassinated in the streets of Jerusalem; another, that he fell in a skirmish with raiders, who had been incited by Nebuchadnezzar to desolate the neighborhood of Jerusalem; another, that he was enticed to the camp of the king of Babylon, and there treacherously murdered; but he died as he lived, dishonorably and miserably.

(b) *Jeconiah.* His was a reign, like Napoleon's after his return from Elba, of one hundred days. He was eighteen when he was called to the throne, and he occupied it for three months and ten days (2 Chron. 36:9); but in that brief time he was able to show the drift of his character.

"He did evil in the sight of the Lord." His mother, Nehushta, daughter of Elnathan, whose hands had been imbrued in the murder of Urijah, and the strong heathen party who dominated the policy of the court, between them molded the young monarch to their will.

Jeremiah uttered words of awful significance. Passing through the streets he showed the marred linen waistband, and foretold the doom of the king and queen mother. "Sit down," he cried, "in the dust, for the crown of royalty shall be rolled from your brow to the ground. The cities in the south country, the beautiful flock of towns and villages, are already in the hands of the invader; and the whole land shall shortly be carried into captivity, because of the abominations, the pollution, the idolatries that have been perpetrated on the hills of the field." Then, coming to closer dealings with the royal pair, he said that Coniah would be given into the hands of them that sought his life, and of those of whom he was afraid; that Jehovah would cast his mother and himself, like a despised broken vessel, into another country, where they were not born; that there they would die; and that there would be no return to the land they loved (13:18–21; 22:28–30).

Thus, too, it befell. Such was the bitter fierceness of the Chaldeans, who were again besieging the city to punish Jehoiakim's perfidy, that nothing would appease them but the surrender of the persons of the king and his mother. There was no alternative; and so, Josephus tells us, a sad procession was formed and, through a gateway—which afterwards bore the king's name, but was bricked up so that none might pass by a path which had been the scene of such a disaster—the king, his mother, the nobles and officials, went forth to the Chaldean camp, and sat down on the ground, their persons robed in black and their faces veiled. By this time Nebuchadnezzar had returned from fighting against Pharaoh-Necho, who had marched to the relief of his ally but had finally been quelled; and he received in person the submission of the royal fugitives (2 Kings 24:7–16).

The plundering of the city followed. The Temple was stripped of its gold and treasures. All the princes, and the mighty men of valor, the craftsmen and the smiths, the king's harem and court officials, were manacled in long lines and torn from their beloved country, which the majority of them were never again to behold. Ezekiel was one of that sad procession; and it seemed as though a pitiful wail arose from the whole country—from Lebanon, and Bashan, and Abarim—as the exiles wended their way to their distant destination. And the prophet wept sore, his eye ran down with tears because the Lord's flock was taken captive.

(c) *The prophets.* The prophets were a large and influential class. Dating from the days of Samuel, their schools had poured forth a succession of men, who occupied a unique position in the land as the representatives of God. But in the degenerate days of which we are now writing, when the kingdom of Judah was rapidly tottering to its fall, they seem to have been deeply infected by the prevailing vices of their time. They were, as Isaiah says, "dumb dogs which could not bark." Greedy and drunken, lazy and dissolute, dreaming, lying down, and loving to slumber, they denied the Lord, and said, when Jeremiah spoke, "It is not he." They had become wind, and the word of God was not in them (Isa. 56:9–12; Jer. 5:12–13).

It must have been very painful for Jeremiah to oppose them, and counteract their influence on the people; but he had no alternative. His heart was broken, and his bones shook; he was in a stupor like a drunken man, and like a man whom wine had overcome, for both prophet and priest were profane; and in God's own house wickedness was rife. Listen to these terrible words, spoken in the name of Jehovah, "In the prophets of Jerusalem I have seen a horrible thing: they commit adultery, and walk in lies; they strengthen also the hands of evil doers, that none doth return from his wickedness; they are all of them unto me as Sodom, and the inhabitants thereof as Gomorrah" (23:9–14).

Jeremiah entreated his people not to hearken to these men, who spoke the vision of their own heart and not out of the mouth of the Lord. Their fatal crime was to live on the traditions of the past and to encourage even those who walked in the stubbornness of their hearts, by assuring them that no evil would come on them. They deliberately set themselves to lessen the power of Jeremiah's appeals and protestations by the promulgation of their own lying dreams, as though they, and not he, were party to Jehovah's secrets.

Matters came to pass shortly after the deportation of Jeconiah. Hananiah, of Gibeon, which was one of the priestly settlements, rose up and publicly contradicted Jeremiah when he was speaking in the Temple, in the presence of the priests and of all the people. Using the holy name of Jehovah, he declared it had been divinely revealed to him that in two years Jeconiah, and all the captives, and all the sacred vessels which Nebuchadnezzar had taken away, would come again. Instantly Jeremiah spoke up from amid the crowd. "Amen," he cried; "would that it might be so; would that Jehovah might bring again the captivity: but it shall not be; nay, it cannot be, without canceling words that have been uttered by him through the prophets before me, and of old."

Not content, however, with his words, the false prophet snatched from Jeremiah's shoulders the wooden yoke which he carried for the purpose of perpetually reminding his people and the neighboring nations that they must serve the king of Babylon until the appointed time had gone. He broke it in two, saying that similarly God within two years would break Nebuchadnezzar's yoke. Jeremiah did not prolong the altercation, but privately told Hananiah that the yoke of wood would be replaced by one of iron, and that he was causing the people to trust a lie. "This year you shall die," he said, as he turned away; and two months later the false prophet was a corpse.

(d) *The surrounding nations.* On two occasions Jeremiah protested against a combination of the surrounding nations to resist the growing power of Babylon, which without doubt was fostered by the neighboring power of Egypt. On the first occasion he said that they would have to drink the cup of the Lord's fury, and on the second, that they must bear the yoke of Babylon. "Now have I given all these lands into the hand of Nebuchadnezzar, the king of Babylon, my servant; and all the nations shall serve him, and his son, and his son's son, until the time of his own land come" (chaps. 25, 27).

All this must have laid the prophet open to the charge of a lack of patriotism: his words weakened the people of the land; his influence withheld them from joining a great league of emancipation. He had no alternative, however, but to be spokesman of that great word of Jehovah, "I will overturn, overturn, overturn."

(e) *The exiles.* The false prophets had suffered the fate of their nation, and were with the rest in captivity; they at once endeavored to raise the hopes of the exiles by prophesying a speedy return. "It is of no use," they said in effect, "to build houses, or plant gardens, or enter into marriage relations. In a short time we shall be back again in Jerusalem." The ringleaders were Zedekiah and Ahab, men of grossly immoral life, who were made an example of by being roasted alive (29:21–23). Still the ferment continued, and the people refused to settle down into contentment with the conditions of their captivity.

Jeremiah therefore wrote a letter which was entrusted to two men of high rank, friendly to himself, whom Zedekiah, the uncle and successor of Jeconiah, sent to Babylon with assurances of his fidelity. "Yield to the will of God" was the burden of the letter. "Build, plant, settle." "Seek the peace of the city whither God has caused you to be carried away captives, and pray unto the Lord for it—for in the peace thereof shall ye have peace." When Shemaiah, one of these false prophets, heard this letter, he wrote off in hot haste to Zephaniah, who was now high priest, and demanded that the prophet should be put into stocks, and his head into a collar, as a madman. The high priest, however, contented himself with reading the letter to Jeremiah, who replied by sending a second letter to the exiles, assuring them that God would punish Shemaiah and his seed, so that he would not have a son to perpetuate his name, and would not see the good which could come at the end of the predestined time (chap. 29).

These denunciations were fraught with terror; and equally terrible was the fate which befell these men. It may be said, "Surely they were patriots, eager for the deliverance of their people. They were fanatical enthusiasts, not intentional criminals. They mistook their hopes for revelations." But it should be remembered that they were also convicted of immoral and evil lives. Their sins had blunted their perceptions of the divine voice, while their words pandered to their people's sins and encouraged them in their lewd idolatries. It was as vicious and fallen men, as well as false prophets, that they incurred the awful woes which befell them, both from the lip of the prophet and the hand of the Almighty.

2. HIS COADJUTOR. While Jeremiah was exercising this ministry of destruction in utter loneliness and isolation, his heart must have often misgiven him. Remember that he loved his country with all the passionate patriotism of which the Jewish nature was capable, and which expresses itself so plaintively in the Book of Lamentations. Matthew Henry says, "It is not easy to preach Christ crucified in a crucified spirit." But Jeremiah did a harder thing. Though for forty years he was constantly in antago-

nism with the sins and vices of the people, the fountain of tears within his soul seems never to have dried up or become frozen over. He preached the terrors of Sinai with the pathos of Calvary.

It was just because he loved so much that he suffered so keenly. And this may comfort others in their dark sorrow and despair for their fellows. They say that their natures are too tender and affectionate and that they feel everything too keenly, as though to infer that they would wish to have been clothed in tougher skin, and cast in a rougher mold. But surely it would be a fatal mistake to barter a tender heart with its faculty of suffering for a callous one without that liability. "Our sorrow," says Carlyle, "is the inverted image of our nobleness. The depth of our despair measures what capability and height of claim we have to hope. Black smoke, as of Tophet, filling all your universe, it can yet by true heart energy become flame and brilliancy of Heaven. Courage!"

You fear to love, lest you may have to suffer; but, ah, how infinitely you lose! You may have an immunity from one sort of pain; but you certainly incur the pain of a selfish, mean, and miserly soul. You miss the valleys of shadow; but you also miss the heights of transfiguration. You save your life; but you lose it. Suppose that Jeremiah had put away the heavenly summons, and had lived in the sequestered ease of Anathoth: he might have secured a respectable and peaceable life, but Jehovah would never have spoken to him; the Unseen and Eternal would never have unfolded to his vision; he would never have felt the supreme satisfaction of knowing that he had done his best; he would never have shone like a star amid the darkening clouds of Jerusalem's fall; he would have missed the hero's crown, the Master's "well done," and the exceeding great reward.

And God sent him an ally and comrade. In the heart of the exiles, Ezekiel arose, uttering the same messages, though clothed in the superb imagery of his gorgeous imagination. He too denounced his people's sins, advised them to settle in the land of exile, and spoke of the certain doom of the people and city. In the mouth of these two witnesses every word was established. Like well-attuned instruments, they symphonized—as our Lord said kindred souls must when they ask concerning some heavenly gift. They were like the two olive trees and the two candlesticks, standing before the Lord of the earth. They had power with God and man, shutting the heaven, turning the waters into blood, and smiting the earth with a curse. So the beast made war with them, as he always will. Theirs was no easy task, for they were hated by those whom their words tormented. But God has long since called them to his throne, where they stand in the foremost rank of those who, having fulfilled the will of God, have received his welcome and reward.

3. THE NEED FOR THIS MINISTRY.

(a) *It must be applied to the unconverted.* For lack of it much gospel effort fails. Of what use are appeals to come to Jesus until the sinner has been led to see the awful peril which he has incurred? Of what avail to extol the balm of Gilead until the soul has heard and accepted the diagnosis of its fatal condition? Of what advantage to offer a seat in the lifeboat, so long as the sailor is full of confidence in his ship and is unaware of its crazy and unseaworthy condition? One of the most important ministries of the servant of God is to destroy false confidence, to pull down refuges of lies, and to show the utter futility of venturing on the sea of eternity in any other craft than that which Christ launched from the cross of Calvary.

It is a great mistake to heal the wound of the heart too lightly. The consolations of the gospel are very well, but they must be withheld until men have seen their state before God and have been held over the mouth of the bottomless pit of their own sin. The greatest revivals always begin in a thorough preaching of the Law, pressing home its demands upon the consciences of the ungodly. Nor is it enough to dwell in general denunciation; we must particularize, until conscience cries, "You are the man!"

(b) *It must be applied to those who lack assurance.* When men say that they cannot believe, it is probably because they are harboring some evil thing in their hearts, or are conscious of some unrepaired wrong in their lives. These must be dealt with. There must be the righting, so far as possible, of ancient injuries, the restitution of ill-gotten gains, the seeking of forgiveness, the adjustment of wrong. The fixed purpose to do this, when an opportunity presents itself, will be sufficient to remove the stumbling block to faith, which will gush out with the sparkle and song of an imprisoned brook. The inability to realize acceptance with God very often points to something that is grieving the Spirit; and at such times the searching ministry of probing and testing and demolition is invaluable.

(c) *It must be applied in the higher attainments of the divine life.* As our obedience grows, our light will grow. And in the growing dawn, we shall become aware of evils that have passed without our notice. The Holy Spirit will lead us to discriminate between the wrong and the right, and reveal what may be hindering us. Then as he destroys one subterfuge after another, ploughs up the fallow ground, disinters the buried secrets, reveals us to ourselves—we may gratefully accept his ministry, which destroys to build, which overthrows to plant, which leads us through the grave that he may minister eternal life. Nor must we overlook the responsibility of exhorting one another, of urging to repentance, and so much the more as we see the day approaching.

16

JEREMIAH'S GRANDEST ODE

(JEREMIAH 51)

God spake and gave us the word to keep;
Bade never fold the hands, nor sleep
'Mid a faithless world—at watch and ward,
Until Christ at the end relieve our guard.
By his servant Moses the watch was set:
Though near upon cock-crow, we keep it yet.

Browning

IT was a very deserted Jerusalem in which Jeremiah dwelt, after king Jehoiachin, his household and court, princes and mighty men of valor, had been carried off to Babylon. It was impossible to take ten thousand of those that constituted the bone and muscle of the nation, without leaving an attenuated and weakened residuum. Still, the fertility and natural resources of the land were so considerable as to give hope of its comparative prosperity, as a trailing vine dependent on Babylon (Ezek. 17).

Mattaniah, the third son of Josiah—who was a boy of ten years of age when tidings came of the awful catastrophe at Megiddo, but who was now in his twenty-first year—was called to the throne by the conqueror, and required to hold it under a solemn oath of allegiance, which was asseverated and sanctioned by an appeal to Jehovah himself. It was as though the heathen monarch thought to make insubordination impossible on the part of the young monarch, since his word of honor was ratified under such solemn and august conditions—conditions which under similar circumstances the heathen king would probably have felt binding and final. Alas! How often heathen men have attached an importance to religious appeals which has shamed religious professors! And how often they must have marveled that we could so lightly disregard them (2 Chron. 36:13; Ezek. 17:13).

At the instance of his conqueror, the young king took the name Zedekiah, "the righteousness of Jehovah." It was an auspicious sign; every encouragement was given him to follow in the footsteps of his illustrious father. And throughout his reign he gave evident tokens of desiring better things. But he was weak and irresolute, lacking the strength of purpose necessary to assert himself for good amid the confused counsels that agitated his court. He respected Jeremiah, but did not dare publicly to espouse his cause, showing him his royal favor by stealth.

Meanwhile the kingdom was violently agitated by rumors from every side, which encouraged the hope that ere long the power of Babylon would be broken, and the exiles return. These thoughts were rife among the exiles themselves, as we have seen; they were diligently fostered by the false prophets, who gladly fell in with the current of the popular wish; and there seem to have been various political considerations which favored the expectation of a speedy reversal of conditions that chafed the proud Jewish heart beyond endurance.

About this time there was a revolt in Elam against Babylon. What if this should spread until the empire itself became disintegrated! But Jeremiah, by the voice of God, said: "It shall not be; the bow of Elam shall be broken; her king and princes destroyed, her people scattered toward the four winds of heaven" (49:34–39).

Then there was the seething discontent of the neighboring peoples who, though they had accompanied the invader as allies, were eager to regain their independence and desired to draw Judah into one vast confederacy, with Egypt as its base. "No," said Jeremiah, "it must not be; Nebuchadnezzar is doing the behest of Jehovah; all the nations are to serve him, and his son, and his son's son" (27:6–7). Perhaps it was at Jeremiah's suggestion that Zedekiah at this time made a journey to Babylon, to pay homage to his suzerain and assure him of his fidelity.

All through the troubles that followed, Jeremiah pursued the same policy. He asserted that the state of the captives in Babylon, as compared with that of the remnant at Jerusalem, was as good figs to bad (chap. 24); when Pharaoh's army produced a temporary diversion, and compelled the Chaldeans to draw off, he said that they would certainly return, set fire to palace and Temple, and burn the city (chap. 37); and his policy was so well-known among the Chaldeans that in the final overthrow they gave him his life, and allowed him to choose where he would dwell (chap. 40).

Often it must have seemed to his choicest friends as though his advice were pusillanimous and wanting in the courage of faith. Did he really favor Babylon above Jerusalem? Was he traitorous to the best interests of his people? But if they ever entertained such questionings, they must have been suddenly and completely disillusioned when he summoned them to hear the tremendous indictment he had composed against Babylon in the early months of Zedekiah's reign, together with the graphic description of its fall. A copy of this prophecy was entrusted to Seraiah, the chief chamberlain, who went in the reign of Zedekiah to Babylon with instructions that he should read it privately to the exiles; and then, weighting it with a stone, cast it into the midst of the Euphrates, with the solemn words that must have thrilled the bystanders, "Thus shall Babylon sink, and shall not rise again, because of the evil which God will bring upon her, and her might shall wax faint" (51:59–64).

1. THE PROPHECY OF THE FALL OF BABYLON.

(a) *The glory of Babylon.* In glowing imagery Jeremiah depicts her glory and beauty. She had been a golden cup in the hand of Jehovah; his battle-axe and weapons of war. Her influence was carried far and wide. She dwelt by many waters, rich in treasure, and the wonder of the earth. Like a mighty tree, she stretched her branches over the surrounding lands. Queen of the nations, she was at ease and thought to see trouble no more. "Is not this great Babylon," her greatest monarch cried, "which I have built for the royal dwelling place by the might of my power, and for the glory of my majesty?"

(b) *The divine controversy.* The Almighty had used her for great purposes of disintegration, doing among the nations much the same sort of work that the icebergs did among the rocks of the primitive world, or that the frosts do each winter in pulverizing the dust of the earth. But she had abused, for unrighteous and selfish ends, the power which God had entrusted to her. Her execution of the divine decrees had been cruel in the extreme. The track of her armies had been marked with ruthless and wanton bloodshed. She had floated to the eminence of another Ararat, on the waters of another flood—an ocean of human suffering. And therefore Jehovah set nets for her and caught her as a wild beast. He opened his armory and brought out the weapons of his wrath.

But God was especially against Babylon for her treatment of his people. The inhabitants of Zion are introduced, crying, "The king of Babylon has devoured us, he has crushed us, and has filled himself with our delicacies. The violence done to me and mine be upon Babylon." Therefore the Most High would take up their cause and take vengeance on their behalf. "As Babylon caused the slain of Israel to fall, so at Babylon shall fall the slain of all the earth; for the Lord is a God of recompenses, he shall surely requite."

(c) *The summons to her foes.* The standard is reared, and around it, at the sounding of the trumpet, the nations gather. The wild tribes of Ararat and Armenia are there, the kings of the Medes, the governors thereof, and all the lands of her empire. The sure-footed shaggy horses of the mountaineers are like the rough locusts that fill the land with their countless multitudes. Sacrifices are offered to propitiate the gods of battle; and the tide of invasion begins to flow against and around the massive walls of the city. The very earth trembles beneath the weight of the armaments and the tread of the troops. "Behold!" the prophet cries, "a people cometh from the north; and a great nation, and many kings shall be stirred up from the uttermost parts of the earth. They lay hold on bow and spear; they are cruel, and have no mercy; their voice roareth like the sea, and they ride upon horses; every one set in array, as a man to the battle, against thee, O daughter of Babylon" (50:41–42, R.V.).

(d) *The attack.* The archers invest the city on every side, so that none may escape. They are bidden to shoot at her, and not spare their arrows. Now the battle-shout is raised and an assault is made against her walls. See! She submits; she gives her hand in token; her bulwarks are fallen; the bars of her gates are broken through; her walls are thrown down; the mighty men of Babylon have ceased to fight; their might has failed; they have become as women. Lo, the fire breaks out amid her dwelling places. The messengers, running with similar tidings from different quarters of the city, come to show the king of Babylon that the fords are in the hand of the foe, and that the city is taken.

(e) *The overthrow of the city.* Then the captured city is given up to the savage soldiery. Nameless wrongs are inflicted on the defenseless and weak. There is plunder enough to satisfy the most rapacious. Her granaries are despoiled; her treasuries ransacked; her stores winnowed.

All the captive peoples who had been held by her in cruel bondage go free, and especially the Jews. "Let us forsake her," they cry, "and let us go every one into his own country; for her judgment reaches unto heaven, and is lifted up even to the skies."

And now her cities become a desolation, a dry land, and a desert, a land wherein no man dwelleth, neither doth any son of man pass through; but the jackals dwell there, and it lies waste from generation to generation, as when God overthrew Sodom and Gomorrah and the neighbor cities thereof.

Such were the predictions of Jeremiah concerning the greatest city which perhaps the world has ever seen, and which was then rising to the zenith of her power and glory. Seventy years were to pass before his words would be fulfilled, but history itself could hardly be more definite and precise. Those who can compare this prophecy with the story of the fall of Babylon, and with the researches of Layard, will find how exactly every detail was repeated, even to the burning of the reeds in the river bed, the meeting of post with post on the night of its fall, the deep stupor with which the fumes of wine had dazed the brave men of Babylon, and the utter desolation which for centuries has reigned over her site.

"They drank wine, and praised the gods of gold, and of silver, of brass, of iron, of wood, and of stone. In the same hour came forth fingers of a man's hand, and wrote over against the candlestick, upon the plaster of the wall of the king's palace. In that night Belshazzar the Chaldean was slain, and Darius the Mede took the kingdom."

2. BABYLON THE GREAT. In every age of the world, Babylon has had its counterpart. Over against the line of Seth, with its reverence for God, was that of Cain, where arts and science were cradled and nurtured. Babel's tower cast its shadow over the primitive races of mankind. Over against Shem was Ham; over against

Abraham, Chedorlaomer; over against Israel, Nineveh; over against Jerusalem, Babylon; over against the Church, Rome; over against the New Jerusalem, Babylon the Great; over against the Bride of the Lamb, the scarlet woman, riding upon the beast. Where God has built up his kingdom, the devil has always counterfeited it by some travesty of his own.

Jeremiah comforted his heart amid the desolations, which fell thick and heavily on his beloved fatherland, by anticipating the inevitable doom of the oppressor. And his words, read amid the exiles of Babylon as they sat beside the rivers and wept, and hanged their harps upon the willows, may have inspired that marvelous outburst of faith, and patriotism, and undying hatred—

> O daughter of Babylon, thou art to be destroyed;
> Happy shall he be that rewardeth thee as thou hast served us.
> Happy shall he be that taketh and dasheth thy little ones against the rock.

In the same way, throughout the persecutions of the empire when paganism made her awful attempts to stamp out Christianity—and afterwards amid the horrors of Inquisition, when the Roman Catholic Church sought to extinguish the true light of the gospel, which in no age has been without witnesses—the suffering children of God have turned to the Book of Revelation to read the doom of that anti-Christian power which, under the guise of paganism or of papalism, always sets itself against God, and is urged on by the undying hatred of the devil. Her fate is described in words that strongly recall those of Jeremiah. She too had the golden cup, and was drunk with blood, and reigned over the kings of the earth. She too is destroyed by a combination of those that had owned her sway. A voice is heard bidding God's people come out from her, lest they be enmeshed in her overthrow. It is rendered unto her as she rendered, and double is mingled into her cup. As Seraiah cast a stone into the Euphrates, so a strong angel casts a great millstone into the sea, saying, "Thus with a mighty fall is Babylon, the great city, cast down, and shall be found no more." And her site becomes the haunt of demons and a hold of every unclean and hateful bird—the voice of harpers and minstrels forever silenced, the light of the household lamp forever quenched, the sound of the millstone forever still.

Prophetic students have always identified this great persecuting power with Rome, the city of the seven hills; and if this interpretation be correct, without doubt, in the millennial age her site will be as desolate as that of Babylon has been for more than two thousand years. But one is disposed to enlarge the scope of the prophecy and to believe that every form of anti-Christian power, whether systems of false philosophy, structures of ancient superstition, or gigantic wrongs like the drink traffic and the opium trade, shall wither and die before the all-conquering might of Emmanuel, who was manifested to destroy the works of the devil. He must reign until all enemies are put beneath his feet. Then shall be heard in heaven the voice of a great multitude, as the voice of many waters and as the voice of mighty thunders, saying, "Hallelujah! For the Lord our God, the Almighty, reigns."

Let us strengthen our confidence in the certain prevalence of good over evil, of the Church over the world, and of Christ over Satan, as we consider the precise fulfillment of Jeremiah's predictions concerning the fall of Babylon. "So let all your enemies perish, O Lord: but let them that love you be as the sun when he goes forth in his might."

3. OUR OWN BABYLON. Each heart has its special form of sin to which it is liable, and by yielding to which it has been perpetually overthrown. How bitter have been your tears and self-reproach! How you have chafed and foamed beneath the strong iron bit of your tyrant! How hopeless your struggles to escape from the tormenting

net, whose meshes refused to break, while every plunge only entangled you more tightly in its folds!

But there is a deliverance for you, as for those weak and misguided but suffering Jews. How exactly your life history is delineated in theirs! They were the children of God; so are you. They might have lived in an impregnable fortress of God's covenant protection; so might you. They forfeited this by their disobedience and unbelief; so have you. They tried to compensate for the loss of God's keeping power by heroic resolutions and efforts, and by alliance with neighboring peoples; so have you. They utterly failed, and were crushed as a moth in a child's hand; so has it been with you. They almost renounced hope; this, too, is your case—you hardly dare hope for deliverance. But as God saved them by his own right hand, so will he save you. And as Babylon was so utterly quelled that it ceased to be an object of alarm, so God is able so entirely to deliver you that you shall no more fear or be afraid—you shall see the bodies of your taskmasters dead upon the seashore.

Accept these rules, if you would have this blessed deliverance.

(a) *Put out of your life all known sin.* Are there vows that never ought to have been made? Recall them! Are there wrongs that lie back in the past which can be righted? Right them! Are there secret habits and practices which eat out your heart? Be willing to be set free, and deliberately tell God so. So far as you are concerned, put away the idols that have provoked God to jealousy.

(b) *Entrust the keeping of your soul to God.* You cannot control it, but he can. He made you and must be able to keep you. One of his angels has power enough to bind the devil; surely then the Lord of all angels can deliver you from the accursed demons that make sport of you. If Christ in his human weakness cleared the Temple, he must be able to drive the foul things from your heart; and when once they are out, it will be easy for him to keep them out. In his ascension, he was raised above all the principalities and powers of darkness, and you were raised with him, too, if you only knew it; certainly the living Christ can tread your lion and dragon beneath his feet. You cannot, but he can. Put the case deliberately, thoughtfully, calmly into his hand. Do not say, "I will try"; but, "I will trust." Do not look at your faith, but at him. Do not cry, "Help me!" for that implies that you are going to do some and he some, and your part will inevitably vitiate all; but cry, "Keep me!" thus throwing the entire responsibility on him.

(c) *Reckon that the Almighty Saviour accepts your deposit at the moment of your making it.* As it leaves your hand, it passes into his. Be sure that he has undertaken it all for you. Do not try to *feel* that he has, but *reckon* that he has. Do not go over and over the act of committal, to see whether it was rightly done. Make it as well as you can, or ask him to take what you but ineffectively transfer. Never doubt that he reads your motive and desire, even though you fail to do as you would; and that he accepts the eager willing for the perfect doing. Then steadfastly resist every suggestion to doubt him. Dare to say a hundred times a day, "Jesus is able to keep that which I have committed to him: I am a worm, weak, witless, worthless; but the Son of God has me in his safe keeping; he has delivered, he does deliver, and I am persuaded that he will deliver yet." You may have no glad emotion, no song of victory, no share of ecstasy; never mind, lie still, and trust God. The lion may roar all around, but the weary, tired sheep will lie within the fold, absolutely safe, because the Shepherd interposes his mighty keeping between it and every dreaded ill.

17

HOW A REED STOOD AS A PILLAR

(JEREMIAH 24, 34, 37)

Thou wast alone through Thy redemption vigil,
   Thy friends had fled;
The Angel at the garden from Thee parted;
   And solitude instead,
More than the scourge or cross, O Tender-hearted!
   Under the crown of thorns, bowed down Thy
     head.

But I, amid the torture and the taunting,
   I have had Thee!
Thy hand was holding my hand fast and faster,
   Thy voice was close to me:
And glorious eyes said, "Follow Me, thy Master,
   Smile as I smile thy faithfulness to see."
              Mrs. Hamilton King

TO a sensitive nature it is an agony to stand alone. By a swift and unerring instinct such a soul can detect what is in men's hearts; and when it knows intuitively that the sympathy for which it yearns is dried up like a summer brook, that interest has changed to indifference and warmth of friendship to the coldness of disdain—whether in organized society or in the great world of human life—its energy ebbs, and its native power of influence is frozen at its spring. To many, the sense of being esteemed and loved is the very breath of life. They would scorn flattery, and the adulation of wealth or fashion; they are quite content to dwell among their own people; but they are so constituted as to require an atmosphere of sympathy for the full forth-putting of their powers.

Many strong and stalwart souls, cast in a heroic mold, have no experience of this sensitive and tender disposition. It is well that they have not. They were born to be the discoverers, the pioneers, the soldiers of the race—theirs the ribs of iron and the nerves of steel, theirs the courage which mounts higher on opposition and ill-will. They will never realize the cost at which those do their work and bear their testimony who have much of the woman in their nature, with its faculty of insight, its warmth of emotion, its keen sensitiveness to praise or hate, its yearning for sympathy, the smile of approbation, the kind word of cheer.

Jeremiah was one of the latter class—tender, shrinking, sensitive, with a vast capacity for emotion, strong to hate and therefore to love, not consituted by nature to stand alone. But herein let us adore that grace which stepped into his life and, for forty years, made him a defensed city, an iron pillar, and brazen walls against the whole land—against princes, priests, and people. They indeed fought against him, but could not prevail, because God was with him. He outlasted all his foes and maintained the standard to life's end. And this marvelous endurance and steadfastness of spirit was nowhere so conspicuous as during the last months of his nation's independence. We must tell part of this story in this chapter that none may miss its helpful inspiration, because, if the presence of God could do so much for him, and for so long, it is sufficient for the weakest child of God that may read these words.

1. JEREMIAH'S ATTITUDE TOWARDS THE KING. We gain much information concerning the situation at Jerusalem during

the reign of Zedekiah from the pages of Ezekiel—who, though resident in the land of the exile, faithfully reflected, and in prophetic vision anticipated, what was transpiring in the beloved city to which his thoughts were incessantly directed. His prophecies are most valuable and interesting when read in this light.

Zedekiah, as we have seen, on ascending the throne, bound himself under the most solemn sanctions to be loyal to the supremacy of Babylon; and there is no doubt that, at the time, he fully intended to be faithful, the more especially as, at Nebuchadnezzar's command, he took the oath of allegiance in the sacred name of Jehovah. But he was weak and young, and wholly in the hands of the strong court-party that favored an alliance with Egypt and the casting off of the Chaldean yoke.

Two years before the catastrophe befell, Ezekiel clearly foretold what was about to happen. He foresaw the embassy sent to Pharaoh requesting horses and people, and asked indignantly, "Shall he prosper? Shall he escape that doeth such things? Or shall he break the convenant, and be delivered?" And he followed up his bitter remonstrances by the awful words, "As I live, saith the Lord God, surely in the place where the king dwelleth that made him king, whose oath he despised, and whose covenant he brake, even with him in the midst of Babylon he shall die. Neither shall Pharaoh with his mighty army and great company be a help to him in the war" (Ezek. 17:11–21).

Jeremiah, as we know, earnestly dissuaded both king and princes from entering into the alliance which was being advocated between Judah and the neighboring states; and he insisted, in the face of the false prophets, that the residue of the vessels left by Nebuchadnezzar in the Temple certainly would be transported, as the rest had been, to Babylon, if they persisted in the mad project (chap. 27). Notwithstanding all these remonstrances, however, the confederacy was formed; and in a fatal moment Zedekiah renounced his allegiance to the king of Babylon.

Then it befell precisely as Ezekiel had foreseen. Stung to the quick by the perfidy and ingratitude of the Jews, who had so persistently and obstinately outraged him, Nebuchadnezzar gathered a vast army, having resolved to make a public example of them to surrounding peoples by the swiftness and mercilessness of his vengeance. "A sword, a sword, it is sharpened, and also furbished: it is sharpened that it may make a slaughter; it is furbished that it may be as lightning. Cry and howl, son of man: for it is upon my people, it is upon all the princes of Israel. They are delivered over to the sword with my people: smite therefore upon thy thigh" (Ezek. 21:8–17, R.V.).

The king of Babylon comes to the junction of the ways—this to Jerusalem, that to Rabbah, the chief city of Ammon. He consults the usual signs of divination, which point him to the assault of Jerusalem, with battering rams, and mounts, and forts. And as he takes the road to the doomed city, the voice of Jehovah is heard bidding the prince of Israel, whose day is come, to remove the mitre and take off the crown because Jehovah was resolved to "overturn, overturn, and overturn." Then, as though to justify the awful sentence, there is given an enumeration of the crimes which were making the streets of Jerusalem red with blood and foul with impurity. It is altogether a terrible description of the state of things in the city during those last years of Zedekiah's reign. A bitter experience for Jeremiah, whose soul must have been sore vexed from day to day, in seeing and hearing their lawless deeds (Ezek. 21:18–27; 22:1–16).

At last, in December, 591 B.C., the siege began. On the approach of Nebuchadnezzar, the confederacy had melted away and Jerusalem was left alone, an island amid the roaring waves of Chaldean armies. But the citizens had laid in a good store of provisions and were expecting daily the advance of Pharaoh-Hophra, with the cavalry of Egypt, to raise the siege.

At this juncture, Zedekiah sent two well-known men to Jeremiah, to ask whether Jehovah would not interpose for his people as he had done in the great days of the past; as, for instance, when he destroyed the host of Sennacherib in a single night. It must have been a trying ordeal to the prophet. One conciliatory word might have averted the dislike of princes and people, given a bright glint of popularity and hero worship, and obliterated the charges of mean-spiritedness and lack of patriotism that were freely leveled at him. Why should he not be the Isaiah of this new siege? Why not arouse and encourage his people to indomitable resistance and heroic faith? Why not blend his voice with those of the prophets that foretold a certain deliverance, and so acquire an influence over them, which might be used ultimately for their highest good?

It is not impossible that such considerations passed before his mind. But if so, they were immediately dismissed. "Then said Jeremiah to them, Thus shall you say to Zedekiah: Thus says Jehovah, the God of Israel, Behold, I will turn back the weapons of war that are in your hands, with which you fight against the king of Babylon, and against the Chaldeans, which besiege you without the walls, and I will gather them into the midst of this city. And I myself will fight against you with an outstretched hand and with a strong arm, even in anger, and in fury, and in great wrath. And I will smite the inhabitants of this city, both man and beast—they shall die of a great pestilence. And afterward, says the Lord, I will deliver Zedekiah, king of Judah, and his servants, and the people, even such as are left in this city from the pestilence, from the sword, and from the famine, into the hand of Nebuchadnezzar, king of Babylon: and he shall smite them with the edge of the sword; he shall not spare them, neither have pity, nor have mercy."

He followed up these terrible words by saying that the only way of safety was to go forth to the Chaldeans, who were now investing the city on every side. All who stopped in the city would die of sword, pestilence or famine. They would be accounted as figs not fit to be eaten, and destined to be cast away as refuse. But those who went forth and surrendered themselves to the king of Babylon would save their lives (21; 22:1-9; 24).

Yet once again, when the siege of Jerusalem was in progress, and every day the air was full of the cries of the combatants, the heavy thud of the battering rams against the walls, and the cries of wounded men borne from the ramparts to the tendance of women—Jeremiah went fearlessly to Zedekiah with the heavy tidings that nothing could stay the sack and burning of the city, since God had given it into the hands of the king of Babylon; and that he would surely be taken and behold him face to face. "He shall speak with thee mouth to mouth, and thou shalt go to Babylon" (34:1-7).

At the same time, rolling across the desert waste and reverberating like a funeral knell, came the terrible voice of Ezekiel: "Woe to the bloody city! Heap on the wood; make the fire hot; then set it empty upon the coals thereof, that the rust of it may be consumed. I the Lord have spoken it. I will not go back, neither will I repent" (Ezek. 24:1-14).

2. HIS ATTITUDE TOWARDS THE SLAVE-OWNING JEWS. It is not impossible that Jeremiah's vehement words of reproof aroused the deeply drugged conscience of his people; and they resolved, at the suggestion of Zedekiah, to make some reparation for their sins, and at the same time strengthen their garrison, by setting free their slaves. This was done at a solemn convocation, specially summoned in the Temple; and the national resolve was ratified before God with the most sacred rites. A calf was cut in two and the princes of Judah, the princes of Jerusalem, the eunuchs and the priests, and all the

principal people, passed between the parts of the calf, as much as to say, May God part us in two, as this beast is, if we turn back from our vow to emancipate our brethren and sisters, Hebrews and Hebrewesses, who are enslaved.

Great joy spread through hundreds of hearts—a body of stalwart defenders was raised for the beleaguered city. Best of all, the nation had done right in the eyes of the Lord. Two months or so passed when, to the unbounded joy of the citizens, the attacks of Nebuchadnezzar became less frequent; the lines of the besieging army thinned; and presently the tents were struck and the whole host moved off. How immense the relief when the crash of catapult and ram ceased and the population pent up so long within their walls could go freely forth! This diversion was caused by the approach of Pharaoh's army. The Jews thought that they would never see their foes again and must have derided Jeremiah mercilessly. They also repealed the edict of emancipation and caused the servants and handmaidens whom they had let go to return to their former condition.

In that tumult of national rejoicing, when the prophet's words seemed falsified, when the fear they had inspired turned to increased hatred against the man who had spoken them, and when he seemed cast off and disowned by Jehovah himself, it must have needed uncommon faith and courage to raise a bold and uncompromising protest. But he did not swerve by a hair-breadth from the path of duty. The infatuation of his people, their treachery to their plighted oath, the disappointment and sufferings of the enslaved, and the honor of Jehovah so ruthlessly contemned—all compelled him to speak out. "Behold, saith the Lord, I proclaim liberty to the sword, to the pestilence, and to the famine. And I will give the men that have transgressed my covenant into the hand of their enemies, and their dead bodies shall be for meat unto the fowls of the heaven, and to the beasts of the earth. And Zedekiah king of Judah, and his princes, will I give into the hand of the king of Babylon's army, which are gone up from you. Behold, I will command, saith the Lord, and cause them to return to this city; and they shall fight against it, and take it, and burn it with fire, and I will make the cities of Judah a desolation, without inhabitant" (chap. 34).

It needed no common moral courage and sense of the presence of God to dare to speak such words; they must have brought down on the devoted head of the lonely prophet storms of abuse. How easy to ridicule him when it seemed so sure that the false prophets were right, and he wrong! His opponents would be proportionately indignant as the voice of conscience, not yet quite silenced, protested that he was speaking the very word of Jehovah.

3. HIS ATTITUDE DURING THE INTERVAL OF RESPITE. The city was delirious with joy. The Chaldeans had withdrawn; Pharaoh would prove more than a match for them; they would not return. The thunder cloud had broken—there was nothing to fear. But Jeremiah never changed his note. It seemed like a raven's croak amid the songs of spring birds. Very depressing! Very unpopular! Very likely to spread suspicion and panic! Only too gladly would he have yielded to the current flowing around him. But he dared not; and when the king sent another deputation to inquire through him of Jehovah, he returned this terrible reply: "Deceive not yourselves, saying, The Chaldeans shall surely depart from us: for they shall not depart. For though ye had smitten the whole army of the Chaldeans that fight against you, and there remained but wounded men among them, yet should they rise up every man in his tent, and burn this city with fire" (37:1–10).

God's prophets had too clear a vision of the issue of the duel between Chaldea and Egypt to be able to buoy up their people with hopes of deliverance. Jeremiah had already foreseen that the daughter of Egypt would be put to shame and delivered into the hand of the people of the north; he had even asked that the tidings of invasion might be published in her principal cities (46:13–28). Ezekiel was not less decisive: "Thus saith the Lord God, I will strengthen the arms of the king of Babylon, and put my sword in his hand: but I will break the arms of Pharaoh, and he shall groan before him with the groanings of a deadly wounded man" (Ezek. 30:24).

Shortly after this, the prophet resolved to take the opportunity, offered by the withdrawal of the Chaldeans, to visit his inheritance at Anathoth, for the purpose of receiving his portion there, perhaps of rent or of some division of tithes among the priestly families, of which he was a member. As he was passing out through the gate of Benjamin, he was recognized by a captain whose family had long been in antagonism with him; and he was not slow to turn the occasion to advantage by repaying a long-standing grudge (37:13). He therefore laid hold on the prophet, saying, "You fall away to the Chaldeans." It was an absurd charge; for the Chaldeans had raised the siege and it was supposed they would not return. The pretext however was sufficient to serve Irijah's purpose and, though it was indignantly repudiated by Jeremiah, he was dragged with violence into the presence of the princes, who were as glad to have their intractable foe at their mercy as the priests to whom Judas offered to betray his Master.

When he had been in a similar plight in the previous reign, Ahikam the son of Shaphan had rescued him, like another John of Gaunt; but he was now dead or in exile. Zedekiah was too weak to interpose to rescue the prophet from the fury of his lords, even if he were acquainted with his peril. And so they adjudged him to the bastinado; forty stripes save one fell from the scourge on his bare back; and he was then thrust into a dark, underground, unhealthy dungeon where he remained many days at the peril of his life.

After a while, Zedekiah, perhaps pricked by remorse or alarmed at the tidings which came from the frontier, sent for him—much as Herod desired to summon John the Baptist from his dungeon to converse with him in his palace halls above. "Is there any word from the Lord?" the king asked, anxiously.

What an opportunity was here for Jeremiah to trim his speech, to put velvet on his lips, and to mitigate the unwelcome truth! Thus he might curry the king's favor and secure for himself deliverance from his intolerable sufferings. But again there was no compromise. "And Jeremiah said, There is. He said also, you shall be delivered into the hand of the king of Babylon."

He then pleaded with the royal clemency for a mitigation of the severity of his sentence, with such good success that he was committed, at the king's command, to the court of the guard, in the immediate vicinity of the palace; he was fed daily with a loaf of bread out of the baker's street, until all the bread in the city was spent. In the meanwhile the army of the Chaldeans, having defeated Pharaoh, returned and again formed their thick-set lines around the city, like a fence of iron, to be drawn closer and closer until Jerusalem fell, like a snared bird, into their grasp.

It is impossible to recite or read this story without admiration for the man who dared to stand alone with God against a nation in arms. It makes us think of Ziegenbalg, the first missionary to the East Indies, standing alone there against the whole force of the authorities, determined to crush his mission in the bud; of Judson, pursuing his work for the salvation of Burma amid the treachery and hostility of the king; of Moffat, going alone and unarmed into the territory of the terrible Africander; of John Hunt amid the ferocious cannibals of Fiji; of John G. Paton, who was preserved amid fifty attempts to take his life. Our sole duty is to see that we are on God's plan and doing his work, to wrap around our souls the sense of his presence, and to keep our ears open to the perpetual assurance, "I am with you, to deliver you." Then we shall leap barrier-walls, pass unscathed through troops of foes, and stand as pillars in his Temple, never to be removed.

18

INTO THE GROUND, TO DIE

(JEREMIAH 32)

All we have willed or hoped or dreamed of good shall
    exist;
Not its semblance, but itself; no beauty, nor good, nor
    power,
Whose voice has gone forth, but each survives for the
    melodist
When eternity affirms the conception of an hour;
The light that proved too high, the heroic for earth too
    hard,
The passion that left the ground to lose itself in the sky,
The music sent up to God by the lover and the bard;
Enough that He heard it once; we shall hear it by and by.
                                Browning

WHILE shut up in the court of the prison, perhaps fastened by a chain that restrained his liberty, Jeremiah received a divine intimation that his uncle would shortly come to him with a request for him to purchase the family property at Anathoth. This greatly startled him because he had so clear a conviction, which he cherished as divinely given, of the approaching overthrow of the kingdom and the consequent desolation of the land. It had been his one incessant message to his people for nearly forty years, that the land must keep her Sabbaths as a judgment for the sins of the people; and now it seemed conflicting and inconsistent to be told to purchase the field at Anathoth, as though it were needed for cultivation. The divine command quite staggered him, and may have made him for a moment question whether there had not been some mistake in the message he had so constantly reiterated in the ears of his people.

He gave, however, no outward sign of his perplexities; but when his uncle's son entered the courtyard with his request, the prophet at once assented to the proposal and purchased the property for seventeen shekels (about £2).* A similar incident is recorded in Roman history. When Rome was being besieged by Hannibal, the very ground on which he was encamped was put up for auction and purchased—a proof of the calm confidence that the Romans possessed of the ultimate issue of the conflict.

In addition to this, Jeremiah took care to have the purchase recorded and witnessed with the same elaborate pains as if he were at once to be entering on occupation. Not a single form was omitted or slurred over; and ultimately the two deeds of contract—the one sealed with the more private details of price, the other open and bearing the signatures of witnesses—were deposited in the charge of Baruch, with the injunction to put them in an earthen vessel and preserve them. They were probably not opened again until the return from the captivity, but we can well imagine how strong a rush of emotion and confidence must have been inspired as the men of that day perused the documents.

But Jeremiah was not a sharer in that glad scene. He did as God bade him, though the shadow of a great darkness lay upon his soul from which he could only find relief, as the Lord on the cross, in recourse to the Father. Indeed, at this point of his life, he resembled the hidden vessel which contained within it the charter of the nation's deliverance. He was an earthen vessel indeed, but he contained heavenly treasure. He fell into the ground to die, as the seed does which holds at its heart a principle of life that can only express itself through death and can only bless men when its sowing, amid the depression and decay of autumn, has been complete.

1. HOURS OF MIDNIGHT DARKNESS. It is only in service that anything reaches its fullest life. A bit of iron is condemned to solitude and uselessness until it becomes part of a great machine. A grain of wheat, hidden for three thousand years in a mummy case, abides alone and only learns the motive and glory of existence when, through death, it learns to weave the chemical juices of the earth, dews, sunbeams, and air, into the fabric of the golden grain. A man who lives a self-contained life, of which the gratification of his own ambition and self-hood is the supreme aim, never drinks the sweets of existence, nor attains his full development. It is only when we live for God, and in doing so, for man, that we are able to appropriate the rarest blessedness of which our nature is capable, or to unfold into all the proportions of full growth in Christ. In the deepest sense, therefore, Jeremiah could never regret that he had given the strength and measure of his days to the service of others. If he had not done so, but had shrunk back from the high calling of his early life, his misery would have been in proportion to the royal quality of his nature and his power to enrich the life of man.

But none can give themselves to the service of others, except at bitter cost of much that this world holds dear. In the words of Christ, the grain of wheat must fall into the ground and die, if it is to bear much fruit. In the case of the wheatgrain, death is necessary to break up the case in which the principle of life lies imprisoned. And in the case of every true life, there must be death to the attractions and indulgences of the self-life, that the soul, being at leisure from itself, may go forth to seek its supplies from God and weave them into nourishing food for the lives of those around. This will explain the privations and sorrows to which Jeremiah was subjected. Death wrought in him, that life might work in Israel and in all who should read the book of his prophecy.

He died to the dear ties of human love. "You shall not take a wife, neither shall you have sons or daughters in this place," was early said to him. The men of Anathoth, of the house of his father, conspired against him. The friends with whom he took sweet counsel, and in whose company he walked to the house of God, betrayed him. What he held in his heart belonged to the race and might not be poured forth within the narrower circle of the home, of priestly temple-duty, or of the little village of Anathoth.

He died to the good will of his fellows. None can be indifferent to this. It is easy to do or suffer when the barque of life is wafted on its way by favoring breezes, or the air thrills with expressions of love and adulation. Then a man is nerved to dare to do his best. And a nature as sensitive as Jeremiah's is peculiarly susceptible to such impressions. But it was his bitter lot to encounter from the first an incessant stream of vituperation and dislike. We have no record of one voice being raised to thank or encourage him. "Woe is me, my mother," he cried sadly, "that you have borne me, a man of strife and contention to the whole earth! I have not lent on usury, neither have men lent to me on usury; yet every one of them curses me."

He died to the pride of national patriotism. No patriot allows himself to despair of his country. However dark the lowering storm clouds and strong the adverse current, he believes that the ship of state will weather the storm. He chokes back words of despondency and depression, lest they should breed dismay. He does not allow his heart to harbor the thoughts of despair that flit across it, and knock for entrance; he drives them away and treats them as traitors guilty of high treason. But Jeremiah was driven along an opposite course. A truer heart than his never beat in human breast. A loftier patriotism than his never hazarded itself in the last breach. His belief in Israel was part of his belief in God. But he found himself compelled to speak in such a fashion that the princes proposed, not without show or reason, to put him to death, because he weakened the hands of the men of war.

He died to the sweets of personal liberty. A large portion of his ministry was exerted from the precincts of a prison. Repeatedly we read of his being shut up and not able to go forth. His friend, Baruch, had constantly to act as his intermediary and interpreter. This, too, must have been bitter to him. His writings abound with references to nature and to natural processes; and the iron fetters of restraint must have eaten deeply into the tender flesh of his gentle heart.

He died, also, to the meaning he had been apt to place on his own prophecies. Up to the moment when Jehovah bade him purchase the property of Hanameel, he had never questioned the impending fate of Jerusalem. It was certainly and inevitably to be destroyed by sword, famine, pestilence, and fire. All that he had ever said in private or public was but the fresh assertion of this bitter fate, with some new touch of pathos, or turn of emphasis. But now the word of God, demanding an act of obedience, seemed to indicate that the land was to remain under the cultivation of the families that owned it.

2. JEREMIAH'S BEHAVIOR. To very few men has it been given so closely to walk along the path which the Redeemer walked during his early life. He was stripped of almost everything that men prize most. But amid it all, he derived solace and support in three main directions.

(a) *He prayed.* Take this extract from his own diary: "Now, after I had delivered the deed of the purchase to Baruch, the son of Neriah, I prayed to the Lord, saying, Ah, Lord God!" Yea, and he was encouraged in this holy exercise; shortly after this incident, when tidings came to him that the houses of the kings of Judah were being broken down to provide materials for the building of an inner line of defense, behind the shell of wall which was nearly demolished by the terrible battering rams, and when his heart was more than ever dismayed, the word of the Lord came to him, saying: "Call unto me, and I will answer thee, and will show thee great and difficult [or inaccessible] things, which thou knowest not" (33:1-5, R.V.).

There is no help to the troubled soul like that which comes through prayer. You may have no clear vision of God. You may be only able to grope your way in the direction where he sits, enshrouded from your view in the thick darkness. You may be able to do little more than recite things which God and you know perfectly well, ending your prayer, as Jeremiah did, with the words, "and behold, thou seest it" (32:24). Nevertheless, pray; pray on your knees; "in everything, by prayer and supplication, let your requests be made known unto God"; and the peace of God will settle down on and enwrap your weary, troubled soul.

(b) *He rested on the Word of God.* The soul of the prophet was nourished and fed by the divine word. "Your words were found," he cries, "and I did eat them: and your words were to me the joy and the rejoicing of my heart." It sounds but hard and cold advice to bid a man in sorrow to read his Bible, but it were impossible to give better. Because, behind the words is the Word; in this garden the Son of Man walks; in this tabernacle the Sun shines in whose beams are health and comfort. How often have God's people turned to the Bible, as the Saviour did in the darkest hours that swept over his soul, and found in a psalm or a chapter the balm of Gilead, the tree of life with healing leaves!

(c) *He faithfully kept to the path of duty.* "And I bought the field." It does not always happen that our service to men will be met by rebuff, ill will, and hard treatment; but when it does, there should be no swerving, or flinching, or drawing back. God's sun shines on the evil as well as the good, and his rain descends on the fields of the thankless churl equally as on those of his children. The fierce snow-laden blast, driving straight in your teeth, is not as pleasant as the breath of summer, laden with the scent of the heather; but if you can see the track, you must follow it. To be anywhere off it, either right or left, would be dangerous in the extreme. And often when the lonely soul has reaped nothing but obloquy and opposition, has been borne to a cross and crucified as a malefactor, it has comforted itself with the prospects of the harvests of blessing which were to accrue to those who had rejected its appeals—just as Pentecost came to those who had been the murderers of Christ.

Such are the resorts of the soul in its seasons of anguish. It casts itself on the ground crying, "Father, Abba, Father"; it stays itself on the word of promise that comes to it in angel garb; it goes forth to yield itself to death, assured that life awaits it and the objects of its choice.

3. COMPENSATIONS. To all valleys there are mountains, to all depths heights; for all midnight hours there are hours of sunrise; for Gethsemane, an Olivet. We can never give up anything for God or man without discovering that, at the moment of surrender, God begins to repay as he foretold to the prophet: "For brass I will bring gold, and for iron I will bring silver, and for wood brass, and for stones iron." We do not make the surrender with any thought of profiting by it; but when we make it, with a single purpose and aim, we learn that when Christ lays a requisition on boat or sailor's time, he returns the boat laden with fish to the water's edge.

Nor does God keep these compensations for that new world, "where light and darkness fuse." It were long to wait, if that were so. But here and now we learn that there are compensations. It may seem a hardship to the man to leave his cell, where he has been immured so long that he dreads the light, the stare of strange eyes, the call for exertion; but when the first stiffness of the joints and novelty of his surroundings have passed off, will he not be compensated? The first movement from the selfish life may strain and try us, the indifference of our fellows be hard to bear; but God has such things to reveal and give as pass the wildest imaginings of the self-centered soul.

So Jeremiah found it. His compensations came. God became his Comforter and wiped away his tears; God opened to him the vista of the future, down whose long aisles he beheld his people planted again in their own land. He saw men buying fields for money, subscribing deeds and sealing them as he had done; he heard the voice of joy and the voice of gladness, the voice of the bridegroom and the voice of the bride, and the voice of them that bring the sacrifices of joy into the Lord's house; he was assured of the advent of the Man, the branch from the root of David, who would sit upon his throne (chaps. 32–33). There was compensation also in the confidence with which Nebuchadnezzar treated him, and in the evident reliance which his decimated people placed in his intercessions, as we shall see. And if he could only know of the myriads who have been comforted by the story of his griefs and by the assurances of his prophecies—red juice pressed into the golden chalice of Scripture by the sorrows that crushed his heart—surely he would feel that his affliction was light and not worthy to be compared with the far more exceeding and eternal weight of glory which it was working out.

So it will be with all who fall into the ground to die. God will not forget or forsake them. The grave may be dark and deep, the winter long, the frost keen and penetrating; but spring will come, and the stone be rolled away and the golden stalk shall wave in the sunshine, bearing its crown of fruit. Men shall thrive on the bread of our experience, the product of our tears, sufferings and prayers.

* This price—perhaps three day's wages—is obviously far below the property's market value. But Hanamel was probably glad to part with it at any price. It has been suggested that the smallness of the sum may have been because the sale conveyed possession only for the unexpired term of a tenancy which was to end with the next year of Jubilee.

The literal Hebrew is "seven shekels and ten [pieces of] silver," though there is no ground for thinking that there is any difference in value between the coins and bullion so described. The precise sum fixed, and perhaps even the form in which the sum is stated, may have originated in a wish by Jeremiah to connect in this way the two numbers ten and seven, which when multiplied together produce the number which he had fixed for the years of captivity in Babylon.

19

THE FALL OF JERUSALEM

(JEREMIAH 38–39)

Among the faithless faithful only he;
Among innumerable false, unmoved,
Unshaken, unseduced, unterrified,
His loyalty he kept, his love, his zeal;
Nor number, nor example with him wrought
To swerve from truth, or change his constant mind,
Though single. From amidst them forth he pass'd,
Long way through hostile scorn, which he sustain'd
Superior, nor of violence fear'd aught;
And with retorted scorn his back he turn'd
On those proud tow'rs to swift destruction doom'd.
                                                    Milton

DURING those long dark months of siege, probably the only soul in all that crowded city which was in perfect peace, and free in its unrestrained liberty, was Jeremiah's. Tethered as he was by an iron chain to the wall of the court of the guard, he passed beyond the narrow confines of the enclosure to the great age that was to be—when Judah would be saved and Jerusalem would dwell safely, known by the name THE LORD OUR RIGHTEOUSNESS. And amid the cries of assailants and defenders, unbroken by the thud of the battering-rams, deep as the blue Syrian sky that looked down upon him, was the peace of God that passed the understanding of those that thronged in and out, to and fro, between the city and the royal palace.

1. THE HORRORS OF THE SEIGE. It lasted in all for about eighteen months, with the one brief respite caused by the approach of Pharaoh's army; and it is impossible for us to estimate the amount of human anguish which was crowded into that fateful space. Some conception of the suffering may be gathered from the words with which Ezekiel anticipated it. As in a mirror, coming events were forecast: the caldron, full of the choicest flesh, hanging over the swift fire until it was consumed; the vision of the iron pan encircling the sun-burnt brick, as the iron legions of Chaldaea would engirdle the beleaguered city; the meager measure of wheat, barley, beans, lentils, millet and spelt, dealt out in measure day by day, but barely sufficient for the prophet's sustenance. The barley cakes mingled with cow's dung, abhorrent to the taste, yet greedily devoured; the stealthy preparation of his household stuff for removal; and the stealing out at night from his house by a hole in the wall, with covered face and laden shoulder—all these spoke with a vividness, which no words could equal, of the horrors of that siege (Ezek. 4).

Imagine for a moment the overcrowded city into which had gathered, from all the country round, the peasantry and villagers who, with such of their valuables as they had been able hastily to collect and transport, had sought refuge, within the gray old walls of Zion, from the violence and outrage of the merciless troops. If wandering tribes, like the sons of Rechab, were induced for once to break the tradition of their nomad life, to shelter themselves within the city enclosure, how much more would the terrified populations scattered in slight habitations over the hill country count it politic to do the same! This mass of fugitives would greatly add to the difficulties of the defense by their demands upon the provisions which were laid up in anticipation of the siege and by overcrowding the thoroughfares and impeding the movements of the soldiery.

The incident referred to in our last chapter, of the demolition of a portion of the royal palace to provide materials for an inner line of defense, is a specimen of many another episode in that intense effort of Zedekiah and his people to hurl back the tide of merciless hate and thirst for blood that broke day after day around the battlements—much as the long ocean wave sends its surges up against a reef of rock and casts its splintered forces high in air. Here there was a scaling party which must be flung back on their ladders; there, an attempt to run a mine which must be intercepted; now tidings came that a portion of the wall, which had been long exposed to the battering rams, showed signs of weakness and must be built up from within; and yet again precautions must be taken against fire flung in missiles, or flights of arrows or stones cast by catapults. For no single hour could the defenders relax their vigilance. A council of princes must have been in perpetual session, fertile in resource, swift to meet the craft or the courage of the foe. And all the time the stock of provisions was becoming less, and the store of water diminishing, as in the case of Malchiah's dungeon, leaving nothing but wet mud.

So much for the earlier months of the siege; but as the days passed on, darker shadows gathered. It was as though the very pit of hell added in human passion the last dread horrors of the scene. The precious sons of Zion, comparable to fine gold, lay by scores in the recesses of the houses, broken like earthen pitchers, the work of the hand of the potter! The women became cruel, and refused to spare from their breast for their young the nutriment they needed for themselves. The tongues of the sucking babes became so dry and parched that they could no longer cry. Young children, whose weakness constituted a first claim, asked for bread and asked in vain. Highly nurtured maidens searched over the dung-heaps, in hope of finding something to stay the craving of hunger. The nobles lost their portly mien and walked the streets like animated mummies. The sword of the invader without had fewer victims than that which hunger wielded within; and, as the climax of all, pitiful women murdered their own little babes and soddened them to make a meal. Finally, pestilence began its ravages; the foul stench of bodies that men had no time to bury, and that fell thick and fast each day in the streets of the city like autumn leaves, caused death, which mowed down those that had escaped the foe and privation. Ah, Jerusalem, who stones the prophets and sheds the blood of the just— this was the day of the overflowing wrath and fury of Jehovah! No human hand lit the flame; no mere human hate was accountable for sufferings so complex and so terrible. You, O God, have slain priest and prophet in your sanctuary; youth and age in the streets. You have slain them in the day of your anger; you have slaughtered and not pitied.

And as Jeremiah waited day after day, powerless to do other than listen to tidings of woe that converged to him from every side, he resembled the physician who, unable to stay the slow progress of some terrible form of paralysis in one he loves better than life, is compelled to listen to the tidings of its conquests, knowing surely that these are only stages in an assault which ultimately must capture the citadel of life—an assault which he can do nothing to stay.

2. THE PROPHET'S ADDED SORROWS. In addition to the discomfort which he shared in common with the rest of the crowded populace, Jeremiah was exposed to aggravated sorrows. It would appear that he was constantly reiterating, in the ears of all who passed through the court of the palace, the message which he had previously delivered to the king: that to stay in the city was to incur death by sword, famine or pestilence, while to go forth to the lines

of the Chaldeans was the one condition of life. He lost no opportunity of asserting that Jerusalem would surely be given into the hands of the king of Babylon, and that the king would take it. As these words passed from lip to lip, they carried dismay throughout the city. Men repeated them as they did duty on the walls, met around the bivouac fires, or discussed the probable issues of the siege; and the fact that Jeremiah had so often spoken as the mouthpiece of Jehovah gave an added weight to his words.

It was quite natural, therefore, that the princes, who knew well enough the importance of keeping up the courage of the people, should demand the death of one who was not only weakening the hands of the people generally, but especially of the men of war. In some such way the drowsy sleeper, unwilling to be aroused by the barking of the watchdog, catches up his revolver to shoot him; or the crew, eager for carouse, murders the watchman who warns them off the white surf breaking along a ragged rock-bound shore. The young king was weak rather than wicked, a puppet and toy in the hands of his princes and court. He therefore yielded to their demand, saying, "Behold, he is in your hand—for the king is not he that can do anything against you."

Without delay Jeremiah was flung into one of those rock-hewn cisterns that abound in Jerusalem, the bottom of which, the water having been exhausted during the extremities of the siege, consisted of a deep sediment of mud, into which he sank. There was not a moment to be lost. The life of the faithful servant of God was not to end amid the damp darkness of that hideous sepulchre from which no cry could reach the upper air; and help was sent through a very unexpected channel. An Ethiopian eunuch—who is probably anonymous, since the name Ebed-melech simply means "the king's servant"—with a love for God's cause, sweetly prophetic of the way in which Gentile hearts would be opened to welcome and forward the gospel throughout the world, hastened to the king, then sitting to administer justice at one of the gates of the city. The eunuch remonstrated with him and urged him to take immediate steps to save the prophet from imminent death.

Always swayed by the last strong influence brought to bear on him, the king yielded as easily to his faithful servant, who was probably the custodian of his harem, as he had done to his lords; he bade the eunuch take a sufficient number of men to prevent interference, and at once extricate the prophet. There was great gentleness in the way this noble Ethiopian executed his purpose. He was not content with merely dragging Jeremiah from the pit's bottom, but placed upon the ropes discarded old clothes and rotten rags, fetched hurriedly from the house of the king; thus the tender flesh of the prophet was neither cut nor chafed. It was an act of womanly tenderness, which makes it as fragrant as the breaking of the box over the person of the Lord. It is not enough to serve and help those who need assistance; we should do it with the sweetness and gentleness of Christ. It is not only what we do, but the way in which we do it, which most quickly indicates our real selves. Many a man might have hurried to the pit's mouth with ropes; only one of God's own gentlemen would have thought of the rags and old clothes. It is very quaint and beautiful, when so much is left untold, that a dozen lines in the Word of God should be given to this simple incident and the hurried advice thrown into the darkness of the lonely prophet by his kindhearted deliverer. "Then they drew up Jeremiah with the cords, and took him up out of the dungeon; and Jeremiah remained in the court of the guard."

From that moment until the city fell, the prophet remained in safe custody. On one memorable occasion the king sought his counsel, though in strict secrecy. Once more, and for the last time, those two men stood face to face: king and prophet; weakness and strength;

representatives, the one of the fading glories of David's race, and the other of the imperishable splendor of truth and righteousness. Once more Zedekiah asked what the issue would be, and once more received the alternatives that appeared so foolish to the eye of sense—defeat and death by remaining in the city, liberty and life by going forth.

"Go forth?" said Zedekiah, in effect. "Never! It would be unworthy of one in whose veins flows the blood of kings. I would expose myself to the ridicule of all who have fled across to the Chaldean lines; for the Chaldeans themselves would deliver me into their hands."

"They shall not deliver you," said Jeremiah, and then began to plead with him, as a man might plead for himself. "Obey, I beseech you, the voice of the Lord, in that which I speak to you; so it shall be well with you, and your soul shall live." Finally, in graphic words he painted the picture of the certain doom the king would incur if he tarried until the city fell into the captor's hands. Instead of the derision of the few Jews that had fallen away, he would then be exposed to the taunts of his wives and children, who would by that time have become allotted to their captors and would seek to win the smiles of their new lords by taunting the fallen monarch in whose smiles they had formerly basked.

In this advice of Jeremiah we are reminded of words repeated by our Lord on five different occasions, and in which he tells us that those who keep their lives lose them, and that those who lose their lives find and keep them. Herein do we find the safe and blessed path: not in husbanding our strength, but in yielding it in service; not in burying our talents, but in administering them; not in hoarding our seed in the barn, but in scattering it; not in following an earthly human policy, but in surrendering ourselves to the will of God. The man of faith judges not after the sight of his eyes, or the judgment of sense; he strikes currents flowing unseen by the world, and acts on suggestions received by direct communication from the Spirit of God, though always through the Word of God and consistent with the loftiest dictates of sanctified common sense.

The weakness which was the ruin of Zedekiah is revealed in his request that Jeremiah would not inform the princes of the nature of their communications and would hide the truth beneath the semblance of truth. It is difficult to pronounce a judgment on the way in which the prophet veiled the purport of his conversation with Zedekiah from the inquisitive questions of the princes. There is an appearance of evasion in his reply, which seems a little inconsistent with the character of the prophet of Jehovah. At the same time, the princes had no right to interrogate him, and he was not obliged by his duty to them to tell the entire truth. We are under no obligation to gratify an impertinent curiosity; but we must be very careful to be transparent in speech and in act, and to be utterly true when we profess to be telling the whole truth to those who have a right to know. In the present case, the prophet shielded the king with a touch of chivalrous devotion and loyalty—which was probably the last act of devotion to the royal house—to save that for which he had poured out his heart's blood in tears and entreaties and sacrifices for nearly forty years.

3. THE FATE OF THE CITY. At last a breach was made in the old fortifications and the troops began to rush in, like an angry sea which, after long chafing, has made for itself an entrance in the sea wall and pours in turbulent fury to carry desolation in its course. The kings of the earth, and all the inhabitants of the world, could never have believed that the adversary and the enemy would enter into the gates of Jerusalem; yet so it befell. Then the terrified people fled from the lower into the upper city; as they did so, their homes were filled with the desolating terror of the merciless soldiery.

A hundred different forms of anguish gathered in that

devoted city, like vultures to the dead camel of the desert. Woe, then, to the men who had fought for their very lives! But woe more utter and agonizing to the women and maidens, to the children and little babes! War is always terrible, but no hand of historian dare lift the veil and tell in unvarnished words all the horror of the sack of a city by such soldiery as Nebuchadnezzar and his generals led to war. The wolves of the Siberian forest are more merciful than they. "All the princes of the king of Babylon came in and sat in the middle gate," from which they gave directions for the immediate prosecution of their success upon the terrified people, who now crowded the upper city, prepared to make the last desperate stand.

Late that afternoon the old palace of David was filled with eager consultation. Everything must be done to preserve the royal house, "the breath of our nostrils, the anointed of the Lord." Therefore, it was arranged that, as soon as night fell, Zedekiah and his harem should go forth under the protection of all the men of war, through a breach to be made in the walls of the city to the south; and exactly as Ezekiel had foretold, so it came to pass. "The prince that is among them shall bear upon his shoulder in the dark, and shall go forth: they shall dig through the wall to carry out thereby: he shall cover his face" (Ezek. 12:12, R.V.).

A long line of fugitives, each carrying valuables and essential items, stole silently through the king's private garden, and so towards the breach; and, like shadows of the night, they passed forth into the darkness between long lines of armed men, who held their breath. If only by dawn they could gain the plains of Jericho, they might hope to elude the fury of their pursuers. But all night Zedekiah must have remembered those last words of Jeremiah: "You shall not escape; but shall be taken by the hand of the king of Babylon." "Woe to him that strives with his Maker. Let the potsherd strive with the potsherds of the earth." This was not the first time, nor the last, that man has thought to elude the close meshes of the Word of God.

Somehow the tidings of the flight reached the Chaldeans. The whole army arose to pursue. "Our pursuers were swifter than the eagles of the heaven; they chased us upon the mountains, they laid wait for us in the wilderness; the anointed of the Lord was taken in their pits." That is the lament of Jeremiah; but Ezekiel gives an even deeper insight into the events of that memorable and terrible night. "My net also will I spread upon him, and he shall be taken in my snare; and I will scatter toward every wind all that are round about him to help him, and all his bands" (Lam. 4:19–20; Ezek. 12:13–14).

What happened the next morning in Jerusalem, and what befell her a month after, when the upper city also fell into the hands of the conqueror, is told in the Book of Lamentations. The street and houses were filled with the bodies of the slain, after having been outraged with nameless atrocities; but happier they who perished then than the thousands who were led off into exile, or sold into slavery, to suffer in life the horrors of death. Then the wild fury of fire engulfed Temple and palace, public building and dwelling house, and blackened ruins covered the site of the holy and beautiful city which had been the joy of the whole earth; and the ear of the prophet heard the spirit of the fallen city crying:

> Is it nothing to you, all ye that pass by?
> Behold and see if there be any sorrow like unto my
>   sorrow which is done unto me,
> Wherewith the Lord hath afflicted me in the day of his
>   fierce anger!

All who passed by clapped their hands at her; they hissed and wagged their heads at the daughter of Jerusalem, saying, Is this the city that men called the perfection of beauty, the joy of the whole earth? All her enemies opened their mouths wide against her; they hissed and gnashed their teeth; they said, We have swallowed her up. Certainly, this is the day that we looked for; we have found it; we have seen it. The Lord did that which he devised; he fulfilled his word. He threw down and did not pity; he caused the enemy to rejoice. Foxes walked upon the desolate mountain of Zion (Lam. 2 and 5).

As for Zedekiah, he was taken to Riblah, where Nebuchadnezzar was at this time, perhaps not expecting so speedy a downfall of the city. With barbarous cruelty he slew the sons of Zedekiah before his eyes, that the last sight he beheld might be of their dying agony. He was also compelled to witness the slaughter of all his nobles. Then as a *coup de grâce*, with his own hand probably, Nebuchadnezzar struck out Zedekiah's two eyes with his spear.

It was indeed a subject for an artist to depict, the long march of the exiles on the way to their distant home. Delicate women and little children forced to travel day after day, irrespective of fatigue and suffering; prophets and priests mingled together in the overthrow they had done so much to bring about; rich and poor marching side by side, manacled and urged forward by the spearpoint or scourge. All along the valley of the Jordan, past Damascus, and then for thirty days through the inhospitable wilderness, retraversing the route trodden in the dawn of history by Abraham their great progenitor, the friend of God, while all the nations round clapped their hands. In after years, the bitterest recollection of those days was in the exultation of the Edomites in the fall of their rival city. "Remember, O Lord, against the children of Edom, the day of Jerusalem!" And the one warlike strain of the evangelical prophet is inspired by the hope that the Divine Conqueror would come knee-deep in Idumean blood (Isa. 63:1–6).

Thus God brought upon his people the king of the Chaldeans, who slew their young men with the sword in the house of their sanctuary, and had no compassion upon young man or maiden, old man or ancient, but gave them all into his hand. And all the vessels of the house of God, great and small, and the treasures of the house of the Lord, and the treasures of the king and his princes, he brought to Babylon. And they burned the house of God, and broke down the wall of Jerusalem; and burned all the palaces thereof with fire, and destroyed all the goodly vessels thereof. And those who had escaped from the sword he carried away to Babylon and they were servants to him and his sons.

Years before in the fourth year of the reign of Jehoiakim, as his friend and amanuensis, Baruch, was lamenting the sore tribulation that befell him in executing Jehovah's commissions, Jeremiah had assured him that at least his life would be preserved in the midst of the final catastrophe. "Thus says the Lord: Behold, that which I have built will I break down, and that which I have planted I will pluck up; and this in the whole land. And do you seek great things for yourself? Seek them not: for, behold. I will bring evil upon all flesh, says the Lord: but your life will I give to you for a prey in all places that you go." As Noah was saved from the waters of the flood, and Lot from the overthrow of Sodom, and the early Christians by their flight to Pella from the horrors of the last fall of Jerusalem, so did the faithful Baruch pass unscathed through those awful scenes. The man with the inkhorn had marked him, and the six men with their slaughter weapons touched him not (chap. 45; Ezek. 9).

20

A CLOUDED SUNSET

(JEREMIAH 40–44)

Therefore to whom turn I but to Thee, the ineffable
    Name?
    Builder and maker Thou of houses not made with
        hands!
What! have fear of change from Thee, who art ever the
    same?
    Doubt that Thy power can fill the heart that Thy
        power expands?
There never shall be one lost Good! What was, shall live
    as before;
    The Evil is null, is naught, is silence implying sound;
What was good, shall be good, with for evil so much good
    more;
    On the earth the broken arcs—in the heaven a perfect
    round!

                            Browning

IF the closing verses of the Book of Jeremiah were written by his own hand, he must have lived for twenty years after the fall of Jerusalem; but they partook of the same infinite sadness as the forty years of his public ministry. It would appear that, so far as his outward lot was concerned, the prophet Jeremiah spent a life of more unrelieved sadness than has perhaps fallen to the lot of any other, with the exception of the Divine Lord.

This was so apparent to the Jewish commentators on the prophecies of Isaiah that they applied to him the words of the fifty-third chapter, which tell the story of the Man of Sorrows who was acquainted with grief, and stood as a sheep dumb before her shearers. Of course, in the light of Calvary, we see the depths of substitutionary suffering in those inimitable words which no mortal could ever realize; but it is nevertheless significant that in any sense they were deemed applicable to Jeremiah.

His sufferings may be classed under three divisions: those recited in the Book of Lamentations, and connected with the fall of Jerusalem; those connected with the murder of Gedaliah and the flight into Egypt; and those of the exile there. But amid the salt brine of these bitter experiences, there was always welling up a spring of hope and peace. The prophet was oppressed on every side, but not straitened; perplexed, yet not unto despair; pursued, yet not forsaken; smitten down, yet not destroyed; always delivered unto death, yet one who passed through death into the true life, sure that the Lord would not cast off forever—that though God caused grief, he would have compassion according to the multitude of his mercies.

1. THE DESOLATE CITY. It is only latterly that any question has been raised as to the authorship of the Book of Lamentations. In the text no author is named, and these exquisite elegiacs have descended to us anonymously. But a very old tradition ascribes them to our prophet. In the Septuagint translation, made in the year 280 B.C., the following introduction is prefixed to the book: "It came to pass, after Israel was taken captive, and Jerusalem made desolate, Jeremiah sat weeping, and lamented this lamentation over Jerusalem." To this the Vulgate adds, "in bitterness of heart sighing and crying." The cave in which Jeremiah is said to have written them is still shown on the western side of the city; and every Friday the Jews assemble to recite as his

these plaintive words, at their wailing place in Jerusalem, where a few of the old stones still remain. There is no good reason, therefore, for disassociating the Book of Lamentations from the authorship of Jeremiah.

This being so, what a flood of light is cast upon the desolate scene when Nebuzaradan had completed his work of destruction, and the long lines of captives were already far on their way to Babylon! How many went into exile we have no means of knowing; the number would probably amount to several thousands, principally of the wealthier classes. Only the poor of the people were left to cultivate the land, that it might not revert to an absolute desert. But the population would probably be very sparse—a few peasants scattered over the sites which had teemed with crowds.

The city sat solitary, which had been full of people. She had become as a widow. Night and day it seemed to the eye of her patriot lovers as though she was weeping sore, and her tears were upon her cheeks; the holy fire was extinct upon her altars; pilgrims no longer traversed the ways of Zion to attend the appointed feasts; her gates had sunk into the ground; and her habitations were pitilessly destroyed by fire. How often would Jeremiah pass mournfully amid the blackened ruins! Here was the site of the altar, there of the most holy place. That was the palace of David, this the new palace that Jehoiakim had made for himself, with its wide windows and heavy coatings of vermilion. Yonder was the court of the guard, where the prophet had suffered so many months of confinement, and there, again, was the place where he had so often stood to warn his people of their sins.

Above and around, nature preserved the unbroken round of her seasons and months, of day and night. The old mountains which had stood around the city in the days of David and Hezekiah glowed with the morning light, and softened in the darkening shadows of the night. The sun arose over Olivet and set in the western sea. The panorama of hill and valley, which lay around like the undulations of a sea of rock, spread itself in its accustomed strength and beauty; for Zion had always been beautiful in her situation. But upon the site of the virgin daughter of Zion the stillness of death had fallen, broken only by the cry of jackal and wild dog.

What all this meant to Jeremiah words fail to say. No truer heart ever beat in patriot's bosom. What Phocion felt for Athens, what Savonarola for Florence, what the elder Pitt for England, amid the catastrophes that darkened his latter days—that, in a concentrated form, Jeremiah must have felt and suffered, whose love for country was so intimately bound up with his religious life. Anticipating the words of One who in later days was to sit on the same mountain and look across the valley, he might have said, "O Jerusalem, Jerusalem, that kills the prophets, and stones them that are sent to you! How often would I have gathered your children together, even as a hen gathers her chickens under her wings, and you would not! Behold, your house is left unto you desolate!"

2. GEDALIAH'S MURDER. Nebuchadnezzar and his chiefs had evidently been kept closely informed of the state of parties during the siege of Jerusalem; and the king gave definite instructions to his chief officers to take special precautions for the safety of Jeremiah. When the upper city fell into their hands, they sent and took him out of the court of the guard; and he was brought in chains among the other captives to Ramah, about five miles north of Jerusalem.

In a remarkable address which the captain of the guard made to Jeremiah, he acknowledged the retributive justice of Jehovah—one of the many traces of the real religiousness that gave a tone and bearing to these men by which they are altogether removed from the category of ordinary heathen. "The Lord your God pronounced this evil upon this place, and the Lord has brought it, and done according as he spoke; because you have sinned against the Lord, and have not obeyed his voice, therefore this thing is come upon you."

The chains were then struck from off his fettered hands, and liberty was given him either to accompany the rest of the people to Babylon or to go where he chose throughout the land. Ultimately, as he seemed to hesitate as to which direction to take, the Chaldean general urged him to make his home with Gedaliah, to strengthen his hands and give him the benefit of his counsel in the difficult task to which he had been appointed. Thus again he turned from rest and ease to take the rough path of duty.

Gedaliah was the grandson of Shaphan, King Josiah's secretary, and son of Ahikam, who had been sent to inquire of the prophetess Huldah concerning the newly found book of the law. On a former occasion the hand of Ahikam had rescued Jeremiah from the nobles. Evidently the whole family was bound by the strongest, tenderest ties to the servant of God, imbued with the spirit and governed by the policy which he enunciated. These principles Gedaliah had consistently followed; and they marked him out, in the judgment of Nebuchadnezzar, as the fittest to be entrusted with the reins of government and to exert some kind of authority over the scattered remnant. To him, therefore, Jeremiah came, with an allowance of victuals and other marks of the esteem in which the conquerors regarded him.

For a brief interval all went well. The new governor took up his residence at Mizpah, an old fort which Asa had erected three hundred years before, to check the invasion of Baasha. The town stood on a rocky eminence, but the castle was supplied with water from a deep well. Chaldean soldiers gave the show of authority and stability to Gedaliah's rule. The scattered remnant of the Jews began to look to Mizpah with hope. The captains of the forces which were in the fields still holding out, as roving bands, against the conqueror, hastened to swear allegiance to the representative of the Jewish state. The Jews who had fled to Moab, Edom, and other surrounding peoples, returned out of all places whither they had been driven, and they came to the land of Judah to Gedaliah unto Mizpah.

How glad must Jeremiah have been to see this nucleus of order spreading its influence through the surrounding chaos and confusion; and with what eagerness he must have used all the energy he possessed to aid in the establishment of Gedaliah's authority! The fair dream, however, was rudely dissipated by the treacherous murder of Gedaliah—who seems to have been eminently fitted for his post—by Ishmael, the son of Nethaniah. In the midst of a feast given by the unsuspecting governor, he was slain with the sword, together with all the Jews that were with him and the Chaldean garrison. On the second day after, the red-handed murderers, still thirsting for blood, slew seventy pilgrims who were on their way to weep amid the ruins of Jerusalem and lay offerings on the site of the ruined altar. The deep well of the keep was choked with bodies. Shortly afterwards, Ishmael carried off the king's daughters and all the people that had gathered around Gedaliah, and started with them for the court of Baalis, the king of the children of Ammon, who was an accomplice in the plot.

It was a bitter disappointment; and to none would the grief of it have been more poignant than to Jeremiah, who in the demolition of this last attempt to effect the peaceable settlement of his country saw the irreconcilable antagonism of his people against the reign of the king of Babylon. This he knew must last for at least seventy years.

The people themselves appear to have lost heart—for though Johanan and other of the captains of roving bands pursued Ishmael, delivered from his hand all the captives he had taken and recovered the women and the children, yet none of them dared to return to Mizpah; rather, like shepherdless sheep, harried by dogs, driven, draggled, panting and terrified, they resolved to quit their land and retire southwards, with the intention of fleeing into the land of Egypt, with which they had maintained close relations during the later days of their national history.

They carried Jeremiah with them. They had confidence in his prayers and in his veracity, since his predictions had been verified so often by the event. They knew he stood high in the favor of the court of Babylon. They believed that his prayers prevailed with God. And, therefore, they regarded him as a shield and defense, a noble representative of the highest hopes and traditions of their people, one in whom the statesman, sage and prophet mingled in equal proportion.

Halting at the caravansery of Chimham, whose name recalls David's flight from and return to Jerusalem—the spot where travelers left the frontiers of Palestine for Egypt—the people earnestly debated whether they should go forward or return. They came also to Jeremiah, and asked him to give himself to prayer, that the Lord his God might show them the way wherein they should walk, and the thing they should do. They professed their willingness to be guided entirely by the voice of God, though in this they were probably not sincere. They dealt deceitfully against their own souls by appearing to desire only God's ways; while, in point of fact, they were determined to enter into Egypt.

For ten days Jeremiah gave himself to prayer. Then the word of the Lord came unto him, and he summoned the people around him to declare it. Speaking in the name of the Most High, he said: "If you will still abide in this land, there will he build you, and not pull you down; he will plant you and not pluck you up. Be not afraid of the king of Babylon, for he is with you to save you, and to deliver you out of his hand." If, on the other hand, they persisted in going into the land of Egypt in the hope that they would see no more war, nor hear the sound of the trumpet, nor have hunger of bread, then they would be overtaken there by the sword, the famine and the pestilence; they would be an execration, an astonishment, a curse and a reproach; and they would never again see their native land. As he spoke, he seems to have been sadly aware that during the ten days devoted to intercession on their behalf the prepossession in favor of Egypt had been growing, and that his words would not avail to stay the strong current which was bearing them thither.

So it befell. When he had made an end of speaking all the words wherewith the Lord had sent him to them, the chiefs accused him of speaking falsely and of misrepresenting the divine word. Not willing to accuse him flatly of treachery, they suggested that Baruch, who was still accompanying him as his faithful friend, had incited him to urge the return to Canaan with the view of betraying them into the hand of the Chaldeans for death or exile. So the terrified people pursued their way to Egypt and settled at Tahpanhes, which was ten miles across the frontier.

Almost the last ingredient of bitterness in Jeremiah's cup must have been furnished by this pertinacious obstinacy, which would not be controlled by his word, which resisted his entreaties, and suggested that his advice was tinctured by treachery in their best interests. How terrible that they should malign and misunderstand the man who had spent forty years of consistent public ministry in efforts to save them from the effects of evil counsel, and to recall them to a simple and absolute faith in the God of their fathers!

3. EGYPT.   His life of protest was not yet complete. No sooner had the people settled in their new home than he was led to take great stones in his hand and lay them beneath the mortar in some brickwork which was being

laid down at the entry of Pharoah's palace in Tahpanhes. "On these stones," he said, "the king of Babylon shall set his throne, and spread out his royal pavilion upon them. He shall smite the land of Egypt, kindle a fire in the houses of its gods, and array himself in her spoils, as easily as a shepherd throws his outer garment around his shoulders. The obelisks of Heliopolis will be also burned with fire. To have come here, therefore, is not to escape the dreaded foe, but to throw yourselves into his arms."

Some years must have followed of which we have no record, and during which the great king was engaged in the siege of Tyre, and therefore unable to pursue his plans against Pharaoh. During this time the Jews scattered over a wide extent of territory, so that colonies were formed in Upper as well as Lower Egypt, all of which became deeply infected with the prevailing idolatries and customs around them. Notwithstanding all the bitter experiences which had befallen them in consequence of their idol worship, they burned incense unto the gods of Egypt, and repeated the abominations which had brought such disaster and suffering upon their nation.

Taking advantage, therefore, of a great convocation at some idolatrous festival, Jeremiah warned them of the inevitable fate which must overtake them in Egypt, as it had befallen them in Jerusalem. "Behold," said the faithful prophet, "God will punish Jerusalem by sword, by famine and by pestilence, so that none of the remnant of Judah, which are gone into the land of Egypt to sojourn there, shall escape, or remain, or return to the land of Judah to dwell there."

A severe altercation then ensued. The men indignantly protested that they would still burn incense unto the queen of heaven as they had done in the streets of Jerusalem; and they even ascribed the evils that had befallen them to their discontinuance of this custom. Jeremiah, on the other hand, gray with age, his face marred with suffering, an old man now, did not hesitate to insist, in the name of the God he served so faithfully, that the sufferings of the people were due, not to their discontinuance of idolatry, but to their persistence in its unholy rites. "Because you have burned incense and sinned against the Lord and have not walked in his law, his statutes or his testimonies, therefore is this evil happened to you, as it is this day." He went on to predict the invasion of Egypt by Nebuchadnezzar, which took place in the year B.C. 568, and which resulted, as Josephus tells us, in the carrying off to Babylon of the remnant of Jews who had, against Jeremiah's advice, fled there for refuge. So it was proved whose word should stand, God's or theirs.

Through all these dark and painful experiences, the soul of Jeremiah quieted itself as a weaned babe. When he said his strength was perished, still his expectation was from the Lord. When his soul remembered its wormwood and gall, he recalled to mind the covenant, ordered in all things, and sure; therefore he had hope. The Lord was his portion, and he hoped and quietly waited for the salvation of God. He knew that God would not cast off forever; but though God caused grief, yet he would have compassion according to the multitude of his mercies. He knew that his Redeemer lived, who would arise for his cause, and render a recompense to his foes. He looked far away beyond the mist of years and saw the expiration of the sentence of captivity; the return of his people; the rebuilding of the city; the holy and blessed condition of its inhabitants; the glorious reign of the Branch, the scion of David's stock; the new covenant, before which the old would vanish away. Probably, therefore, his days were not all dark, but aglow with the first rays of the Sun of Righteousness, smiting the Alpine peaks of his holy and loyal spirit. The Comforter must have come to him. God, who comforts those that are cast down, must have spoken words of balm and tender peace. Never yet in the history of the world has

God permitted his servants to sink in unrelieved and hopeless midnight. Unto the upright there always arises light in the darkness. The gloomiest hours that ever brooded over the Son of Man broke up with the cry, "Father, into your hands I commend my spirit."

If these words should be read by some whose life, like Jeremiah's, has been draped with curtains of somber hue, shutting out the glad light of day, who have trodden the path of sorrow and the valley of shadow, let them know that nothing brings men into such intimate relationship with the Spirit of God, and that to none does the Infinite One stoop so closely as to those that are sore broken on the wheel of affliction. It is only when we fall into the ground and die that we cease to abide alone and begin to bear much fruit. Do not try to feel resigned. *Will* resignation. Submit yourself under the mighty hand of God. If you can say nothing else, fill your nights and days with the cry or sob of "Father, not my will but yours be done." Never doubt the love of God. Never suppose for a moment that he has forgotten or forsaken. Never yield to the suggestion of the adversary that the harvests which you are to garner could have been procured at any less cost. As for God, his way is perfect and he makes our way perfect.

Scripture says nothing about the death of Jeremiah. Whether it took place, as Christian tradition affirms, by stoning in Egypt, or whether he breathed out his soul beneath the faithful tendance of Baruch, in some quiet chamber of death, we cannot tell. The Bible makes comparatively little of death scenes, that it may throw into greater prominence the prolonged narrative of the One Death, which has abolished death. God's chief interest is focused on the life and work of his servants. What they did, said, and suffered is more to him than how they surrendered their lives at his bidding. Indeed, to know how a man has lived is to make us largely indifferent of information regarding his last hours. The sculptured column projects its shaft in perfect symmetry upward from the earth, though we may not be able to follow it because the mass of waving verdure veils it from our gaze. But we know it is beautiful and in perfect harmony with all we behold.

But how gladly did the prophet close his eyes upon the wreck that sin had wrought on the chosen people, and open them on the land where neither sin, nor death, nor the sight and sound of war break the perfect rest! What a look of surprise and rapture must have settled upon the worn face, the expression of the last glad vision of the soul as it passed out from the body of corruption, worn and weary with the long conflict, to hear the "Well done!" and welcome of God.

The memory of Jeremiah was cherished with exceptional reverence. It seemed to the restored people as if his tender spirit were watching over their interests. Later, the struggles of Judas Maccabaeus were cheered by the thought that Jeremiah had come to succour him; it was believed that the prophet continued in heaven the intercessions for which he had been so famous on earth. And then, in the days that preceded the second siege of Jerusalem, it was supposed that Jeremiah had reappeared in the person of the Son of Man (Matthew 16:13–14).

This book was produced by the Christian Literature Crusade. We hope it has been helpful to you in living the Christian life. CLC is a literature mission with ministry in over 45 countries worldwide. If you would like to know more about us, or are interested in opportunities to serve with a faith mission, we invite you to write to:

Christian Literature Crusade
P.O. Box 1449
Fort Washington, PA 19034